Look to
Your Left

Akron Series in Contemporary Poetics

Akron Series in Contemporary Poetics
Mary Biddinger and John Gallaher, Editors
Nick Sturm, Associate Editor
Jordan McNeil, Associate Editor
With thanks to Syliva Moran

Mary Biddinger, John Gallaher, eds., *The Monkey & the Wrench: Essays into Contemporary Poetics*
Robert Archambeau, *The Poet Resigns: Poetry in a Difficult World*
Rebecca Hazelton & Alan Michael Parker, eds., *The Manifesto Project*
Jennifer Phelps and Elizabeth Robinson, eds, *Quo Anima: Innovation and Spirituality in Contemporary Women's Poetry*
Kristina Marie Darling, *Look to Your Left: A Feminist Poetics of Spectacle*

Look to Your Left

A Feminist Poetics of Spectacle

Kristina Marie Darling

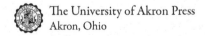 The University of Akron Press
Akron, Ohio

ISBN: 978-1-62922-120-5 (paper)
ISBN: 978-1-62922-121-2 (ePDF)
ISBN: 978-1-62922-145-8 (ePub)

A catalog record for this title is available from the Library of Congress.

The paper used in this publication meets the minimum requirements of ANSI NISO Z 39.48–1992
(Permanence of Paper). ∞

The views contained herein are those of the individual authors and do not necessarily reflect the
views of the editors, the Akron Series in Contemporary Poetics, or The University of Akron Press.

Cover: © Kalina Winska, *Antrakt—Detail*. Duralar and epoxy resin, hardware, approx. 12 x 15 x 14
feet. Used with permission. Cover design by Amy Freels.

Look to Your Left was designed and typeset in Garamond with Mr. Eaves San titles by Amy Freels
and printed on sixty-pound natural and bound by Baker & Taylor Publisher Services of Ashland,
Ohio.

Produced in conjunction with the University
of Akron Affordable Learning Initiative.
More information is available at
www.uakron.edu/affordablelearning/

Contents

An Introduction

THE ESSAYS IN this collection examine, from a variety of perspectives and conceptual standpoints, the ways performative language in contemporary poetry can be politically charged. The poetic text, then, becomes a spectacle, which ultimately renegotiates the power dynamics implicit in the simple act of looking. As the language unfolds before the reader, they are involved and implicated in a revision of what is and what always has been an unequal share of power on the stage of textual authorship and readerly interpretation.

With that in mind, I have chosen the poets whose work is examined here with an eye toward the unique possibilities of performative language for women, poets with a nonbinary gender identity, and writers of color who foreground social justice as a crucial part of their artistic practice. The work of these innovative creative practitioners is contextualized against the writing of poets working within a framework more visibly grounded in a received literary tradition, as opposed to its revision, reconstitution, and inevitable redirection.

Writers like Matthew Rohrer, Ilya Kaminsky, and Andrew Seguin experiment, challenge, and revise as their artistic inheritances loom large. Within the context of this study, texts like *Deaf Republic*, and its rich engagement with international poetry and global literature; *The Others*, and its accompanying New York School influences; and *The Room in Which I Work*, steeped in provocative performances of critical theory; may be approached as conceptual bridges between more mainstream artistic communities that value innovation and those that exist on the periphery due to structural injustices.

The first section of this volume, "Look Again: Renegotiating the Gaze," begins by theorizing women poets who take up the act of looking as an artistic subject, both through actual representation and through performative language as a metaphor. These poets—Victoria Chang, Anne Barngrover, Jessica Baran, Solmaz Sharif, and many others—redirect the gaze to the broken cultural mechanism itself, prompting us to become suddenly and irrevocably aware of the power structures embedded in our ideas about looking, spectacle, and spectatorship. The essays then move to redirect the gaze of theory, considering ways that silence, rupture, and elision can also be performative within this context.

The second section of this essay collection, "The Contemporary Experimental Text as Event," interrogates and pays homage to the artistic legacy of contemporary women, nonbinary poets, and writers of color. By tracing the poetic lineage of contemporary innovators in poetics, I hope to show how the work of early Modernist poets is transformed, and in this process of reinterpretation, made even more just and even more hospitable to conversations about social justice.

The third section of this essay collection, "Unruly Language: Towards a Poetics of Disruption," builds on this discussion of modernism, considering work by women poets, and contemporaries with whom they enter into artistic dialogue, that defies genre categories and readerly expectations of how language should or ought to behave.

Lastly, I have taken the liberty of including an Afterword that addresses feminist issues in the literary community more generally. These essays examine the ways women's writing and women's bodies are constructed within language. Because language is what gives meaning, form, and structure to our experience of the world around us, a revolution in society ultimately begins with our thinking about grammar, rhetoric, and the narratives that circulate within culture.

Lastly, I would like to note that the style of the writing is part of this work's performance. In much the same way that classic texts within a mainstream literary canon are presented without contextual flourishes, the peripheral texts considered here are elevated to that same timeless realm. With that in mind, this work should be approached as intervention, as readerly imperative, and as feminist spectacle in and of itself.

Look Again

Redirecting the Gaze

Victoria Chang's Poetics of Female Spectacle

LIA PURPURA NOTES in "Relativity" that "each thing's / its own partner / each always both, depending on / where you stand." We all glance at ourselves and imagine what the other sees; a thousand possible selves surface. The other's gaze becomes a constant presence within the self, a character in the stories we tell each other and ourselves. Though this imagining might appear to some as an exercise in empathy, it usually replicates the limited, existing ideas that populate our media, rather than imagining our own. As Slavoj Žižek argues, these texts "don't give you what you desire. [They] tell you how to desire."[1] Victoria Chang's collection, *Barbie Chang*, reveals, visibly and poignantly, the ways that "looking" can be symptomatic of what is most broken and dangerous in our culture.

For Chang, tacit beliefs about race, class, and gender reside just beneath the surface of the gaze, dictating the power structures implicit in our looking and the inevitable imbalance of agency and visibility. Chang elaborates on her subjectivity in an interview with Abigail Welhouse for *The Rumpus*: "I think being a poet, period, is isolating, because it's so marginalized in our culture. On top of that, I'm a female poet, which is another sub-segment of an already-marginalized art. And I'm an Asian American female poet, which is even more marginalized." In *Barbie Chang*, what Chang describes as "marginalized" is wedded to perhaps the most recognizable standards of beauty, femininity, and visibility. This is not to say that Barbie is marginalized for her appearance, but rather, the opposite. She occupies a position of privilege and enjoys the luxury of legibility in the eyes of the predominant culture. It is this privilege that Chang undermines, interrogates, and defamiliarizes.

Indeed, this tension—between looking as we understand it and as Chang presents it—is what drives the collection. As the sequence unfolds, Chang suggests that we are the very things people see us as, inevitably, because they are internalized.[2] But we are also defined by our resistance to the archetypes that circulate around us (and within us). She considers the problem of the split subject, the divided self, through both narrative and subtler stylistic choices. Filled with enjambments that enact violence on language and syntax, and rife with cavernous silences, *Barbie Chang* renders us suddenly—startlingly—aware of the warring multiplicity housed within each one of us. "I want to change the ending," she writes, "before this begins" (41).

As a cultural symbol, Barbie represents the ways intellectual activity is coded as masculine, and a vacuous mind as inherently ladylike, a standard against which the speaker constantly measures herself. Play becomes prescriptive, sparking the speaker's awareness of her own looks and their seeming incongruity with a rich and ever-shifting inner life. At the same time, Chang bravely and provocatively acknowledges the pleasures of this particular definition of femininity: "Barbie Chang can't stop watching / the Ellen Pao trial // while the rest of the world wonders / about a plane crash..." (16). For Chang, vacuous femininity has its allure, as the speaker relishes the drama of the televised trial. The testimony describes "Pao falling in love with a man in the office," rather than the rich social, political, and historical implications of her demand for equal pay (16). As we transition from line to line, this kind of escape seems all the more appealing. In light of the book's provocative exploration of race, this passage evokes the simultaneous attraction and terror of internalizing a Westernized standard of beauty. For the speaker of this poem, conformity is a necessary prerequisite to gain power and legibility, but also a pathway to something potentially destructive. In poem after poem, we are presented with a speaker who challenges complicity and engages her humanness. She finds herself "forever frozen in her own form like / a stamp" (17).

In many ways, the poem's formal consistency amplifies—and reflects on—this tension. Presented almost entirely in couplets, Chang's poems certainly present a feminist critique of spectatorship in a literary form that represents a male tradition. Yet such a reading overlooks the uneasy music of the poems, their sonic trepidation, a powerful commentary on the poems' chosen form. Chang writes, "There are lungs in Barbie Chang's / dreams and jeeps in her / lungs the lungs are hard and almost / dead the jeep no longer / runs…" (6). Here her lineation exists in tension with the sentence, the clause, or any familiar unit of syntactic meaning.

These ruptures and aptly timed schisms serve to convey the speaker's sense of dread, an anxiety that renders it difficult to breathe and speak. One might read this angst as the voice's reaction to being placed in a form in which it fits uneasily, a cadence that is uncomfortable in its own adornments and unnecessary ornamentations. This visible unease represents a sharp contrast with the earlier "Barbie Chang Can't Stop Watching," with more natural pauses that punctuate the speaker's narrative of spectatorship: "…men like to take off their clothes / extend their tongues…" (16). Here, we are presented with lineation that mirrors the rhythms of speaking. It is a voice at ease within the language that it inhabits. Chang shows us, through form, that the other's gaze offers both pleasures and perils, both of which preoccupy the speaker of these meaningfully crafted poems.

The book is filled with poems like this, in which the author's deft stylistic maneuvers complicate and question the form, narrative, and artistic tradition from which the work arises. "Barbie Chang hates the status quo," the poet explains, her commitment to social justice shining through each line break, each fractured syntactic unit (30). She shows us that the other's gaze is internalized, perhaps most visibly in the way we inhabit language. After all, these limiting ideas—telling us what beauty, identity, and desire should be—manifest even in the rules that govern our words, as seemingly innocent and necessary as they may be.

Barbie Chang startles us into awareness. Chang's star is rising, and lucky for us, she writes with compassion, grace, and a true ethical sensibility. When read in light of her previous collections, *Circle*, winner of the 2005 Crab Orchard First Book Award, *Salvinia Molesta*, published in 2009 by the University of Georgia Press, and *The Boss*, released by McSweeney's Books in 2013, this volume represents Chang's finest achievement, and her most enlivening work yet. This is not to say that her other work is lacking, but that here, she pushes her unique line of inquiry—which examines questions of otherness, marginalization, and identity—even farther, pursuing these questions with greater boldness and resolve. Rather than affording the reader the luxury of a passive role, which the autobiographical lyric strophes of *Circle* lend themselves to, she holds a mirror to the other, forcing them to look, and to examine their own victimization and complicity.

Anne Barngrover's *Brazen Creature*
Southern Masculinities and the Violence of Spectacle

WILLIAM MICHAEL DICKEY notes that the "ability to punish via the gaze" is quite powerful, especially as it is "internalized by individuals who correct and police their own actions so as not to be seen as criminal or chastised by others" (19). The simple act of looking performs and dramatizes these imbalances of power, indicating who can see and be seen without violating the order of things. These tacit rules are inevitably internalized, and we live with them more in our solitude than in our moments of resistance. As a result, the nascent thought—that almost unconscious impulse toward connection, conversation, and community—is cut short before it has even been fully articulated.

Anne Barngrover's second collection, *Brazen Creature*, navigates these questions of power, self-censorship, and surveillance with a refreshing candor, while fully doing justice to the complexity of this line of inquiry. Presented as a book-length sequence of linked persona-driven pieces, the poems in this stunning collection examine a type of spectatorship particular to the American South, that sprawling expanse of "poison ivy," "muscle and fog." Within the context of Barngrover's regional poetics, an ongoing awareness of being looked upon not only polices, but also isolates. She elaborates in "Hallucinate the House, Hallucinate the Woods,"

> … I wake to a bomb
>> going off inside my own head and the ghosts of flashlights

glow against the windowpanes of my brain—a parasomnia
        so rare doctors won't bother to record. I feel like a wasp

nest nailed to a door…(1)

Here the female speaker subtly suggests through her choice of imagery—the "wasp / nest nailed to a door," the shut "windowpanes," the bomb confined to the inside of her "own head"—the loneliness inherent in being an object of the gaze. Not only is she threatened with scrutiny and erasure—that moment when "there are no stars"—but she is paralyzed by her ongoing awareness of tacit judgment, that "ghost of a flashlight" that finds its way into the innermost rooms of her house. At the same time, solitude becomes a communal endeavor, as the speaker functions as a captive to the neighborhood even in the absence of any other voices, "words," or "sounds."

As the book unfolds, Barngrover's speakers consider the gaze as the product of a community, arising from a complicated matrix of men and women laying claim to visibility within a cultural landscape that threatens to erase some part of them. Frequently offering sketches of characters who populate the Southern towns that the book traverses, Barngrover's writing is perhaps most impressive as it delves into the trauma and precariousness of Southern masculinity. Unlike the speaker of "Hallucinate the House, Hallucinate the Woods," who finds herself hostage to the gaze, these men struggle to hold on to the visibility that has always, irrefutably, been theirs. She explains in "He Hates What I Do,"

…He'd had

a married woman once (*a very poor girl*)
then his boss, two students (*they were sort-of former*).

He'd won a steak dinner

                (*a gentleman's agreement*)

for which housemate would be the first to fuck
their landlord's brown-skinned daughter,

> he bragged to me as he threw a dart
> against a door...(57–58)

Here Barngrover presents the male gaze as a precursor to conquest, a foreshadowing of gendered imperialism. Each woman who is beheld by the man in this poem, whether the "sort-of former" students, the "married woman," or the female "boss," is proffered, in this somewhat disturbing litany, as evidence of his successful performance of masculinity for female onlookers. His romantic conquests become a kind of masculine spectacle, which is presented to the speaker of this poem to no effect. We are made to see that he speaks against the threat of erasure, and a postmodern cultural landscape in which "darts" and "steak dinners" no longer make a man.

For both the men and women who populate this theoretically astute and thought-provoking book, there is an undeniable cruelty implicit in the gaze. This violence could best be described as an unrelenting psychic intrusion, a mediating presence that ultimately shapes our way of being in the world. The cruelty of the gaze arises from a lack of choice, as Barngrover reminds us that we are born into the spectacle that unfolds endlessly before us.

Her work is especially striking when the women she portrays reconstitute and appropriate the politics of the gaze, reframing this unwanted mediation as a source of empowerment. She writes, for example, in "Finding Out the Lie One Year Later,"

> He wants a chimney cowl, a curved stone...
> ...And I'd be a liar
> tonight if I didn't wonder: before fireworks were shaped like flowers,
> if one woman ever thought to make them weapons, and how. (11)

Here Barngrover's female speaker is surrounded by the trappings of conventional femininity: a domestic scene complete with "a chimney cowl," "flowers," and so on. Yet she is no longer captive to the gaze, its implicit rules and politics, or the ongoing threat of judgment from the community she inhabits. Needless to say, she recognizes herself as spectacle, all "fireworks" and flame, but the violence that has been done to her has been turned outward, fully and convincingly weaponized.

This ferocity proves to be contagious. She writes in "The Encounter":

> …I was not fearful,
> though she growled at me as I passed by, brazen
> creature who refused to shrink back into the thrum
> of new evening, into the wild from where she'd come. (76)

Here, and in other poems in this intriguing volume, readers will discover that they are called upon to locate themselves in Barngrover's narrative of power and spectatorship. Through a multifaceted and compassionate construction of narrative, we recognize ourselves in both the "brazen creature" and the "wild" that surrounds her. We realize our own complicity, and our own victimization, and find ourselves better equipped to navigate the "new evening" that surrounds us.

Surveillance, Metanarrative, & the Female Gaze

Solmaz Sharif, Andrew Seguin, & Jessica Baran

IN "EXPANDING THE Gaze: Gender and the Politics of Surveillance," Sandra Lee Bartky argues that for many women, "surveillance, and the self-surveillance prompted by constant observation, is covertly coded as a masculine gaze," evoking the myriad ways that power and disempowerment are internalized. Bartky rightly frames looking as bound up with larger institutional structures of gender, authority, and violence, a sprawling landscape of "dead space" and "battlefield illumination" that is reflected back even when we look at ourselves. The wonder and terror of being seen intrude on even our most solitary moments, dictating the terms of our dreaming, inscribing the boundaries of all that we are willing to imagine.

Three collections of poetry fully do justice to the complex relationship between gender, power, and surveillance. Solmaz Sharif's *Look*, Jessica Baran's *Common Sense*, and Andrew Seguin's *The Room in Which I Work* consider, with impressive technical dexterity, the possibility of creating alternative spaces in language, which resist the gaze of the nation state and deliberately position those in power as textual outsiders. Yet these writers go beyond simple reversals of power, envisioning the complexities of language as a refuge, obfuscation as a "kind of game" in which a genuine ethical sensibility stands to be lost or won. Though vastly divergent in form and approach, these three innovative practitioners share a commitment to poetry as a hypothetical testing ground, where we can reimagine the social order starting with its very foundations: language itself.

This implementation of textual difficulty as a political gesture, as a show of both solidarity and resistance, is perhaps most visible in these writers' approach to syntax. Here, we have clauses that fit together, yet resist any clear causal relationships that we attempt to impose. In the work of Baran, Sharif, and Seguin, we are offered the illusion of cohesion, a wholeness that fractures when we look too closely. As Solmaz Sharif tells us in "Inspiration Point, Berkley," "There is nothing that has nothing to do with this" (32).

⁂

Andrew Seguin's *The Room in Which I Work* is presented as a lyrical history of the camera. Because Seguin's own practice involves both text and image, the narrative reads, in many ways, as a story of literary origin, an articulation of artistic genealogy. Seguin envisions the poetic image and the photographic image as being coeval for modern practitioners, who are reared "in this age" of digitized excess, in which all that darkness "might come home as memory with a scalloped edge."

If the poetic image, as imagined by modern practitioners, shares its origins with the glittering "mechanisms" of surveillance, Seguin prompts us to consider the possibility of reclaiming this vast and far-reaching cultural machinery. Indeed, many of the poems contextualize the photograph as the work of one's hands, a product of skilled labor and artistry. "My camera listens for the sun in woodsmoke," he writes, "its mirror not even / breathing in the dark." Here, the photographic image is humanized, and re-envisioned as an artisanal object, one that is carefully curated, deliberately crafted by the individual citizen's hand. Even more importantly, Seguin calls our attention to photography as a visceral and embodied language, a lexicon unto itself.

He renegotiates, in true Steinian fashion, the relationship between signifier and signified within the exquisite tapestry of visual rhetoric that unfolds throughout his collection. The book is populated by familiar archival material, which Seguin expertly complicates, pairing each of these images with hybrid texts that interrogate, and undermine, their photographic counterparts. "Authority loves fixed points," he explains, offering a self-reflexive commentary on the work's destabilizing effects. Part of the work's difficulty, and its pleasure, is the way that text and image together generate possibility. What's more, *The Room in Which I Work* allows each of these distinct lexicons to interrogate one another, so that the work reads as a conversation about, and between, the two mediums. "Lavender, moss, phosphor, squash," Seguin writes, "from each he asked a secret."

❧

Solmaz Sharif's *Look*, like Seguin's collection, considers the relationship between language and the photographic image. She also examines the ways the rhetoric of surveillance infiltrates our most commonplace social interactions. Here, language, through its implicit hierarchies, its subtle ordering of the world, becomes a means of intruding on, and ultimately shaping, our actions in what we thought were private spaces. Every gesture is revealed as politically charged, whether we fully realize our complicity or not. "This is no innocent passage," she informs us (17).

Sharif elaborates,

> …I see him
> between odd jobs in four different states,
> and on the video our friend shows baba a picture
> of me and asks *how do you feel when you see Solmaz?* (39)

Here, we are made to understand how this awareness of being seen is inevitably internalized. As the book unfolds, Sharif shows us the many forms that this self-surveillance can take, ranging from deliberate spectacle to a kind of unconscious censorship in one's most solitary moments, a silencing that becomes almost second nature. Even more importantly, she reveals the language of surveillance as a presence we rarely recognize, intruding on our psyche, inscribing the boundaries of all that we dare to imagine. We do not realize that the "threshold" we cross has a double meaning, culled from the *Dictionary of Military and Associated Terms*. Likewise, we remain largely unaware that the word "look," in mine warfare, is "a period during which a mine circuit is receptive to an influence."[3]

What is perhaps most provocative about Sharif's work is that she confronts the violence that has been enacted onto language, through language. The words we use are revealed as conduits for various abuses of power, a doorway into the psyche that allows for intrusions, that frightening presence of the other within the most intimate spaces of the mind.

❧

Baran, like Seguin and Sharif, writes against, and in spite of, the mechanisms of surveillance, and the various structures of power that they represent. Through her gratifyingly dense style, and her innovative use of prose forms, Baran proffers language as an opportunity for both complicity and resistance. Here, textual difficulty becomes a gesture of opposition and empowerment. It is the text's intricacy, the sheer labyrinthine quality of its dream-logic, that becomes what Julia Kristeva termed "a revolution in poetic language."

Certainly, Baran's work arises out of the same philosophical problem that Sharif confronts in *Look*, bringing to light the many ways that the mechanisms of violence and power intrude on the psyche through language, that necessary condition of dreaming. And like Seguin, Baran reimagines the relationship between signifier and signified, creating a new lexicon, one that is not implicated by the cultural machinery she resists. Yet her work is marked by an interest in creating an alternative space through poetry, in which language can be fully reimagined, with violence and threat no longer submerged beneath its glittering surface. Baran elaborates, in "Teenage Lust,"

> Reports disturb: teenage lust is waning.
> Graduate dreams, parental affection—
> all fail-safe measures, have, in fact succeeded
>
> in abolishing hallway trysts
> during fundraiser lock-ins. Molly bloom
> in high school undoubtedly drew
>
> Baroque notes to a different Leopold.

What's particularly revealing about this passage is the way narrative convention no longer means what we think it does. We are offered resolution after resolution: "abolished hallway trysts," "a different Leopold," "the fail-safe measures, in fact succeeding." Yet the world around us has come undone. The poems resist conventional logic, becoming a kind a laboratory, a hypothetical testing space for various changes to the order of things. What's more, the poet's hand remains carefully hidden throughout all of this, the pronoun "I" rarely appearing in the collection. We traverse the dystopian space that Baran has created, certain that it is merely façade, that the answer to our questions is stowed behind a locked door. Much like the work of Sharif and Seguin, Baran's collection shows us a provocative reversal of power, calling into question "the assorted fictions" that govern our life in language.

The Literary Text as Performance & Spectacle

Writing by Virginia Konchan, Barbara Tomash, & Julie Doxsee

WHEN THINKING ABOUT how the experience of cultural otherness is internalized, poet Lia Purpura observes the power imbalance implicit in the simple act of looking. For many individuals from historically marginalized groups, the gaze is often symptomatic of all that is broken, dangerous, and problematic in our culture. To be seen is to be subjected to the judgments, assumptions, and normative ideals of the viewer, a subtle presence that we inevitably, in the spirit of *Barbie Chang*, deconstruct, critique, reject.

Purpura suggests in an interview in *Pinch Journal*, though, that "language might repair certain tears in our consciousness, restlessness in our behavior, violence in our attitudes." For Purpura, looking, and its seemingly small violations, is filtered through and woven into language. It is the words we use that structure these interactions, that give form to our perceptions. More often than not, language reinforces these imbalances of power in the hierarchies that it creates, whether through grammar and the causal relationships implied in the ways words are sequenced and arranged, or the gendering of nouns in many languages.

Recent years have seen a proliferation of feminist writers who are taking up these questions about language, spectatorship, and the orders of power implicit in the gaze. After all, these questions only seem to multiply with the Trump administration, the #MeToo movement, and the ongoing violence that comes to light in our community on a nearly daily basis. More now than ever, poets are telling us where to look, as well as refusing, restructuring, and renegotiating the terms of the gaze.

If language structures and gives form to our perceptions, then the words we use inevitably perform and dramatize the implicit politics of looking. And these words are rife with possibility, especially when considering a more mindful, and more ethical, model of spectatorship. Three visionary poets are using performative language to implicate and involve the reader in new ways of thinking about spectacle, in which those who have previously been disempowered assume greater agency and visibility.

☙

Because grammar is the foundation of a society, giving form to various imbalances of power and agency, a revolution in the social order inevitably begins in language. For Barbara Tomash, author of *PRE-*, a feminist poetics involves refusing the gaze; the object that we as readers are beholding is skillfully hidden from view. The effect that this gesture has on the reader is a kind of productive bewilderment, which prompts careful attention to Tomash's innovative textual landscape.

Through her atypical use of typography, Tomash creates her own lexicon. In doing so, she constructs an imaginative world in which language is the object to be regarded, scrutinized, and beheld as spectacle, as show. Tomash forges a new grammar, one that allows for purposeful ambiguity, multiplicity, and a veritable proliferation of meaning and possibility. The gaze is reversed, refracted, and broken open. We are shown the infinite possibilities that had been there, in language, all along. Tomash gives us the familiar shrouded "in mutually unintelligible languages." She shows us all that we once knew burning "to ashes [at] a white crystalline stalk" (19).

Tomash's *PRE-* fittingly blurs the boundaries between elegy and ode, between grammatical construction and deconstruction. Here, each poem is named for a common prefix, including "be-," "trans-," "ante-," and "col-." As the book unfolds, we watch as each poem performs the etymological history, implied relationships, and the causal structures evoked by the prefix, even when isolated from the very thing that it modifies. Tomash writes, for example, in "[col-],"

> to labor together in bones and fibrils : together in paper,
> cloth, or wood : shrink together abruptly and completely :
> fall into a jumbled, flattened mass : a mass of legal
> wreckage : a number of persons : to give way the bridge : (4)

Here we are offered a lexicon in ruins: "bones and fibrils," "a jumble," "a mass of legal wreckage." What is lovely and astonishing here is Tomash's restraint, as so much is left unsaid in this piece. This is fitting as the prefix she is writing about means "with," and Tomash subtly evokes silence and separation, the luminous space between things. As a result of the silence that inhabits this work, poet and reader "labor together" to navigate language without the familiar tools of grammar, narrative, and syntax, to create a vocabulary that is more hospitable and more just.

For Tomash, it is the performative qualities of language that open up these other possibilities for relating and interacting, for positioning the self in relation to the other. She boldly and provocatively eschews narrative, instead juxtaposing vastly different languages and phenomena without attempting to delineate relationality. She gives us "*trans*, over, across + *spirare*, to breathe" all bereft of narrative scaffolding (54). Throughout the work, her diction also ascends and descends in register, spanning a wide range of rhetorics and discourses, though resisting the familiar arc of narrative all the while. The book functions as "a short simple story," but one that is "inconsistent with : a moving point," a textual body that rejects the structure warranted by the readerly gaze (63). The end result is a work devoid of hierarchies, instead challenging the reader to navigate the many textures of language without the most familiar tools for meaning-making. We realize, as soon as the book has closed, the many ways we have been mastered by culture; we recognize our own guilt and complicity as we long for the last clear narrative, the beautiful (and beautifully recognizable) arc of story.

It is what we do not recognize, all that is unfamiliar and strange, that forces us to look again at language and reconsider our place within it. Much like Tomash, Julie Doxsee creates a feminist poetics that refuses the gaze through her gratifyingly dense linguistic constructions. As Western readers, so many of us expect a text that is legible in a very particular way, one that can be understood, mastered, and set aside. Doxsee's *what replaces us when we go*, however, takes the form of impressively intricate prose constructions—grammatically impeccable but that often do not *mean* in the way we think they should. For Doxsee, the interrogation of grammar from within, and the subversion of its implicit causal structures, becomes the spectacle, the thing to be beheld, watched, and gazed upon. "We realized our gazes go to infinity," Doxsee explains (11).

In much the same way that Tomash looks beyond grammar, narrative, and the familiar structures of meaning-making, Doxsee shines a light on the power dynamics implicit in the act of reading, as her text becomes a spectacle that resists the gaze, and the mastery that resides just beneath it. "twenty / sugar-shrunk lips blow kisses / to the stampede of cows left back," Doxsee says (6). Gratifyingly strange and impressively fresh in its reimagining of surrealist influences, this poem resists those who approach the reading act as an opportunity to dominate a writer's voice, who regard interpretation as a chance to arrest the free play of meaning inherent in language. The productive tension between language, imagery, and grammar strikes sparks, raising fascinating questions, as opposed to the answers we are so accustomed to searching for in a narrative.

Doxsee writes, for instance, in "Black Sea,"

> A fly's vibration wakes up
> cone-ear dogs the forest
>
> wide & every morning
> the same choir of howls
>
> tears a vertical chute
> in the mist & fills it
>
> with throat-wet diamonds. (9)

Presented in pristine and orderly couplets, Doxsee's language resists this containment, eschewing the clean logic and linearity implied by the form. The poem is propelled forward by alliteration, assonance, and internal rhyme, rather than the suspense of narrative. In such a way, Doxsee privileges the sonic qualities of language over their semantic qualities, destabilizing the very foundations of the linguistic terrain she traverses. Unlike Tomash, who eschews the structures of grammar almost completely, Doxsee reimagines what is possible within them. We watch as unruly language resists the forms we attempt to impose upon it. What's more, we are mere spectators as what is possible within language expands, opens up, multiplies.

The best poets remind us that grammar contains many possible worlds within it, if we would only be willing to explore what might at first be an unfamiliar linguistic usage. Differing slightly from the work of Tomash and Doxsee, Virginia Konchan's *The End of Spectacle* documents and catalogues the dismantling of old models, which include fairy tales, well-known films, and twentieth-century fashion icons. For her, the postmodern cultural landscape that we inhabit is nothing other than an invitation, a call to action, as the reader has the opportunity to build something beautiful from the "makeshift stage" that has toppled before us over the course of this gorgeously lyrical, skillfully rendered, and subtly philosophical collection. As Konchan herself tells us, "I have a foothold in consciousness, / yet am possessed by the idea of none" (62).

Much like the books by Tomash and Doxsee, *The End of Spectacle* explores, performs, and dramatizes the collapsing of old frameworks for thinking through the relationship between self and other, and between viewer and viewed. Subtly and skillfully, Konchan catalogues the various models of spectatorship that we have inherited from past generations, whether it's the "view from the tower" in a familiar fairy tale, the "façade" of a house that has "evolved from the Queen Anne," or the speaker's "dream" of drawing a "bath of sublime temperature" for her beloved (12–13).

As this taxonomy unfolds before us, Konchan brilliantly calls our attention to the ways spectacle and looking are inextricable from outmoded ideas about gender—in other words, the familiar notion that looking requires an active agent and a passive object. Here, too, the princess who gazes from a high tower, the speaker who "dreams" of pleasing a beloved with all that is "purely decorative" (13), and Coco Chanel in her "bolero jacket" (19) all posit themselves as objects of desire to gaze upon, rather than active agents in the imaginative landscape of the poems.

What is beautiful and astonishing about Konchan's work is that her speakers sense an end to this passive variety of feminine charm, a seismic shift that is met with complex, multifarious, and wide-ranging emotion.

The speakers of her poems also recognize an end to the power inherent in orchestrating the spectacle of desire and desirability, but they also see an unprecedented opportunity: "All hail the end / of spectacle, pieces // of royaume scattered // on the sidewalk" (19).

In the end, this is an invitation that Konchan extends to the reader—in the midst of "hooves pounding, / dust flying, emcee / roaring," she challenges us to build something even more beautiful, a relationship between viewer and viewed that does not exploit or disempower (19). Like Tomash and Doxsee, Konchan's thinking about spectacle resists the mastery implicit in looking, but also recognizes the potential for empowerment and reversals of power.

If language functions as the internalization of power and disempowerment, then the gaze most exemplifies this idea of language as imposed structure, as mediation and intrusion. The words we use give form to the various imbalances of visibility and agency implicit in the simple act of looking. In this respect, language often constitutes the most intimate and lingering abuse of power, a presence that one cannot shake even in solitude. With remarkable skill, dexterity, and grace, Doxsee, Konchan, and Tomash show us that, as Julia Kristeva famously argued, a revolution in the social order begins in poetic language.

"Spare This Body, Set Fire to Another"
Silence as Performance & Sociopolitical Empowerment

IN THE ONE volume of writing that he published during his lifetime, Ludwig Wittgenstein claimed that "the limits of my language are the limits of my world" (149). Grammar, and the rules that govern speech acts, inevitably structure our relationships, determining what can—and what may never—be said between two people. Even in solitude, it is linguistic convention that circumscribes the boundaries of our dreaming, even as we begin to sense that bright expanse that lies just beyond our reach.

Three poetry collections skillfully interrogate the limitations of language, exploring ways that we as readers and creative practitioners can expand the boundaries of what is communicable, giving voice to all that is, as Kaveh Akbar says, "wilding around us" (16). Kaveh Akbar's *Calling a Wolf a Wolf*, Brenna Womer's *Atypical Cells of Undetermined Significance*, and Henk Rossouw's *Xamissa* share a commitment to making audible that which lies at the outermost periphery of language. Though wide-ranging in style and conceptual approach, these writers turn to experimental forms as a means of critiquing linguistic convention, calling attention to its arbitrary limitations. Theirs is a critique that performs and dramatizes its grievances with respect to grammar, and we watch as that "whole paradisal bouquet spins apart" (11).

What is perhaps most striking about these writers' experimentation is the way their gorgeously fractured forms invite silence into the work. As each of these three collections unfolds, we watch as moments of rupture, elision, and interruption gesture at all that lies beyond the printed page. These writers show us that, as Akbar says, "we are forever folding into the night" (6), and they give us, through their bold experimentation, a vocabulary for articulating its "regret" (65), "its spiritual conditions" (60), and its "diamonds" (59).

⁂

Akbar's *Calling a Wolf a Wolf* is structured as a series of linked, persona-driven pieces, many of which make expert use of white space within the line. These seemingly small gaps within the text proper accrue vast, wide-ranging, and unwieldly emotional resonances. "As long as earth continues / its stony breathing, I will breathe," the speaker tells us (39). And in much the same way that Akbar makes us attend to the almost imperceptible rhythms of the physical body, he calls our attention to the space between words, suggesting that the very foundation—of meaning, of speech, of communication—resides there.

We first encounter silence in the work in the first moments of the opening piece, "Wild Pear Tree." Here, the poetic line is literally halved, a gap manifesting in the very center, its form making visible all that is yet unspeakable: "it's been January for months in both directions   frost…" (5). What's perhaps most revealing about this passage is Akbar's use of white space to amplify the limitations of the language we do encounter. Here, we sense a sorrow just beyond the pristine imagery that we are actually given. It is that sorrow that cannot yet be named, that finds a name over the course of the book-length sequence. In these opening lines, however, all that is at that moment unspeakable—addiction, longing, excess and its disappointments—is rendered as a startling absence, and that elision is what gives rise to the wonderfully imperfect and awe-stricken music of these poems.

Silence becomes the driving force of the work, the language merely orbiting around its alluringly absent center. Akbar writes, for example,

> they all feel it   afterwards the others dream
>
> of rain their pupils boil the light black candles
> and pray the only prayer they know   *oh lord*
> *spare this body   set fire to another* (17)

Here Akbar invokes silence as a way of performing and dramatizing time, both literal time and lyric time, that temporality which is measured in emotional, visceral, and psychic duration. It is the sense that time has elapsed ("they all feel it   afterwards") that changes our encounter with the words that do exist on the printed page. But also, it is this sense of time passing that signals all that has been elided by the narrative itself. Here past and present are juxtaposed, and it is the reader's task to create the lovely narrative arc that lends meaning, unity, and form to experience. By gesturing at the arbitrary nature of language, narrative, and their repertoire of forms, Akbar opens up the possibility of alternative models for structuring lived experience. And by the final lines of the poem, we are given one in the deus ex machina that inhabits the final line: "*spare this body   set fire to another.*"

If narrative is a kind of conjuring, an appeal for meaning, structure, or order that may not be immediately apparent, language is the space in which that alterity makes itself known. The meaning that we arrive at through the unwieldly apparatus of grammar is indeed an otherness, a specter that haunts a room that is not its own. What's more, it is the space between words where the ghosts of "corpses" and "chariots," the "blank easels" and "orchids" of memory, actually live, waiting for a body to breathe into.

Like Akbar's *Calling a Wolf a Wolf*, Womer's *Atypical Cells of Undetermined Significance* explores the ways in which silence, rupture, and elision call into question all that resides on the printed page. She takes physical illness and medical trauma as her subject, interrogating the body as a discursive construction, knowable only through our relationship to language. In much the same way that Akbar forces the reader to attend to the space that separates words, and the almost-imperceptible rhythms of the human body, Womer calls our attention to the transitions between the many discrete episodes that comprise the book. For Womer, the female body resides in these apertures, in that bright and liminal place between the various narratives and myths that have been imposed from without.

Presented as an extended sequence of hybrid texts, which shift rapidly between "psychic injury," "emotional shock," and "Lipton iced tea powder mix," Womer's writing mirrors the experience of being a patient through the behavior of its language (32). She actively involves the reader in the struggle to glean meaning in the space between fractured, contradictory, and ultimately incommensurable fragments of text. Womer writes, for example, in "When a Psychic Says We're Soul Mates,"

> Recall how you know the heart,
> and remember the future, the
> brain, the chronic hunger and
> burn; life in a wet summer, loud
> and close—eternal, intolerable.
>
> Number the young. (8)

After this lyrical meditation on the delights and displeasures of the human body, Womer transitions to a prose vignette:

> We drove in the day before Hurricane Isabel with our lives blocking the rear view of our Ford Expedition. There was no available housing…(9)

In the moment between sections, that brief pause, the body shifts from being a site of pleasure (and emotional labor) to a site of endangerment and finally, disconnect, as the speaker manifests as a split subject (with their lives "blocking the rear view" mirror). She dissociates from her physical body, giving voice to a palpable separation. The swift movement between "Hurricane Isabel," "crumbling red brick," and "1970s standards" performs and enacts this disconnect, involving the reader in an impossible task of meaning-making and creating unity from a discontinuous experience. "I found a pair of seagulls caught on two hooks of the same iridescent lure," she writes (16). Here, imagery mirrors the book's philosophical underpinnings.

As we traverse the "trauma," "fatal diseases," and "deal-breakers" that comprise the narrative, Womer shows us that none of these lexicons renders experience more faithfully than the last. Not the "chronic hunger" of the lyric interludes, nor the "categories" articulated in the more scientifically minded sections. Like Akbar, Womer uses silence, rupture, and elision to call into question, and provocatively undermine, what is on the printed page.

Using the same stylistic repertoire, she gestures at the artifice of many conceptual models for understanding the physical body. Much like Akbar's provocative consideration of narrative and syntax, this argument is made through form and technique, rather than in the text proper. As Womer's hybrid sequence progresses, we are made to confront the varying levels of authority and credibility that we attribute to different registers and discourses, which, in this case, range from poetic imagery to medical jargon ("150 viruses, each assigned its own number").

"I wanted to be a mother but only on Sundays," Womer tell us (23). Throughout the collection, lyrical interludes like this one are juxtaposed with medical documents, patient questionnaires, and records of the senses. By transitioning between rhetorical modes in such a way, Womer suggests that the female voice is rarely accepted as a source of knowledge about the body, or a credible vehicle for an explanatory model. Womer implies that facts about the body are often only seen as credible when they arrive in familiar forms, particularly those that populate the medical field and the biosciences. Yet it is in the silences, and the elisions, that these power dynamics become clear to the reader. It is in the apertures that the ethics of the text crystallize. As Womer herself tells us, "You didn't ask for a miracle, but got one anyway" (25).

Rossouw's *Xamissa* continues Akbar's and Womer's exploration of what silence makes possible when articulating a philosophy of language. In the work's "Proloog," he notes that the title of this thought-provoking volume actually derives from linguistic accident:

> Perhaps it was here the urban legend emerged: "Camissa," we thought, meant "place of sweet waters" in the indigenous Khoe language. And the waters the urban legend speaks of have run from Table Mountain to the sea, under the city itself, since before the Dutch ships. An untrammeled toponym, from before the 1652 arrival of the Vereenigde Oostindische Compagnie (VOC), "Camissa" became a wellspring for the cultural reclamation I witnessed in newly democratic Cape Town. In the 2000s, Café Camissa shut down to make way for a real estate agency—a symptom. (1)

Here meaning, and the task of translating, seem straightforward, but begin to unravel and refract over the course of Rossouw's introductory narrative.

This anecdote frames the work beautifully, as the style of the writing skillfully performs this unraveling of narrative continuity.

Formally, the book begins with the semblance of wholeness, and the reader is borne from pristine prose paragraphs to the almost tangible documents of an archive. We are presented with the author's identity documents, and no accompanying information or caption. In an instant, the rhetorical situation of the work changes: the reader shifts from a passive recipient of meaning to an active agent in creating meaning. With that in mind, the space between texts and episodes in *Xamissa* is especially powerful. It is in these bright apertures, the liminal spaces within the text, that the laws of grammar, syntax, and narrative no longer hold. In these brief pauses, the rules of the text, and the rules governing its language and narrative, can be entirely reconfigured.

"Heretofore unseen: / a piece of census again / or a ship's manifest / redacted with ash and / doubt," Rossouw writes (56). Like many passages in *Xamissa*, even the poetic line serves to amplify uncertainty. Just as the pause before "doubt" conveys even the narrator's trepidation, it is the silences in this work that are made to house the weight of history. Much like Akbar, Rossouw envisions silence as the center around which the book's poetics orbit. Just as *Calling a Wolf a Wolf* creates music out of all that cannot, and will not, be said aloud, *Xamissa* envisions the space between languages, histories, and temporal moments as an invitation, that "half-light" beckoning the reader inside what had once been a darkened room.

As the book unfolds, its form—and the silences to which this experimentation give rise—become unruly, even disruptive, when considering the narrative conventions engaged by Akbar and Womer. Here, we are made to walk through the archive that accompanies any subject's life in language. Handwritten ledgers, official documents, and watermarks are juxtaposed with lines of poetry and lyric fragments. "I write the debris number C 2449 on the form / in pencil and wait for the ash in the half-light," Rossouw's speaker tells us (48).

In many ways, it is this movement between documents, "secrets," and "fire" that presents such a provocative challenge to what does exist on the page. Indeed, the transitions between different types of language, and the silence that fills the moments we spend in these liminal textual spaces, allow the reader to fully inhabit the archive in all of its indeterminacy, rather than a neatly structured master narrative. In other words, we encounter language— and the histories contained within it—in a nonhierarchical way. Like Womer's interrogation of medical jargon and the rhetoric of diagnosis, Rossouw erases the judgments, and the arbitrary valuations, that we impose upon different types of language and text. What's left is a "field on fire," a subversion of the politics surrounding the very documents he has gathered (83).

If silence is a gradual undoing, then the space between things makes visible that unraveling. It is the pauses between words that are most danger- ous, as they hold the power to destabilize the text that surrounds them. Rossouw's archival poetics reads as both homage and destruction, a lyric appreciation of the work silence can do (and undo).

When silence becomes a gradual undoing, an unraveling of certainty, there is a violence done by saying nothing. Womer, Akbar, and Rossouw undoubt- edly destabilize many of the rules that govern our lives in language. At the same time, they do so with a true ethical sensibility, as their efforts to inter- rogate, and undermine, linguistic convention are born out of a desire for a way of communicating that's more just and more true. For these poets, silence becomes a form of resistance, as well as a weapon and a relic of all that is holy. By interrogating the space between things, these poets have offered a philosophy of language where anything becomes possible. After all, it is in the liminal spaces that rules no longer hold. It is in the brief pauses between arias that it becomes possible to shift keys. As Rossouw observes in *Xamissa*, "I listen not in silence but in song, a form of interruption" (52).

The Aesthetics of Silence

Ilya Kaminsky's *Deaf Republic* & Donna Stonecipher's
Transaction Histories

CHRIS P. MILLER asserts that "silence is a chronology, a beginning collapsed into the end." For Miller, silence manifests as the first—and truest—form of compression, a charged and dense rhetorical space in which even time folds in on itself. In *Styles of the Radical Will*, Susan Sontag describes this remarkable compression not as a destructive force, but rather, as transcendence, a sure sign of language sublimating into dream, insight, and artistic vision. Approached with these ideas in mind, the gaps between words, lines, stanzas, and prose paragraphs become charged with possibility, a liminal space in which the rules governing speech no longer hold.

Two collections of poetry frame silence not as failure, but as potentiality, transformation, and resistance. Ilya Kaminsky's *Deaf Republic* and Donna Stonecipher's *Transaction Histories* invite a startling absence to inhabit their music, manifesting at turns as fragmentation, omission, wild and unexplained juxtapositions of images, and a careful withholding of narrative context. Yet in both of these finely crafted volumes, the reader witnesses silence transforming from elegy to paean to metaphor and back again, as the space between words is made to hold entire worlds.

Though vastly different in style and scope, these innovative collections, through their innumerable ruptures and elisions, frame listening, especially in a rhetorical space characterized by absence, as a radical and visionary practice. What's more, through an undoubtedly performative approach to language, Kaminsky and Stonecipher involve the reader in a deft performance of this soothsaying, this gradual process of divination and revelation. Each collection, then, reads as a ledger of a consciousness transformed by deep listening. As Stonecipher herself writes, "Aftermath after aftermath after aftermath. Each word was a vault containing the pale blue glass of its history" (63).

⁂

Donna Stonecipher's *Transaction Histories* appear as a series of thematically linked prose vignettes. Yet in the early pages of this collection, the dense, ornately worded paragraphs are perhaps most startling in their fragmentation, as a visible rupture tears at the very center of each piece, its music interrupted, literally halved, by this destructive gesture. Yet this negative space at the very heart of each poem functions much like the "skeleton key" that appears throughout the work, offering a point of entry into the work's potentialities if the reader is attentive enough to unlock them.

"[T]here were locks upon locks in rows," Stonecipher writes, "as in a locksmith's dream, and one key so slippery it kept falling out of her hand into the sky, floating up into the deeps" (3). In much the same way, the intent behind Stonecipher's dense and baroquely lyrical prose constructions seems at first to be elusive. Yet this same certainty often eludes the speaker of the poems herself, as her mind orbits from "the past with its black perfect perfections, its ashtrays and princess telephones" back to the imperfect present as the "glass" falls from her hand and shatters "on the balcony" (3). We realize that we are searching along with the speaker for patterns, convergences, and confluences in the vast sprawling texts of time, history, and culture. The elisions in the very center of each poem, then, offer a space for meaning to accumulate, to take hold in the seemingly random fabric of a shared consciousness.

We come to realize, along with the speaker, that "What's past is never past, but moves from room to room in the blue honeycomb of the brain, or blooms in domes that crown the fretted space of her thinking" (3). Fittingly, as the sequence unfolds across time and history, these gaps disappear from the book's pages, as a gorgeously fractured narrative arc begins to emerge. In such way, a transient unity of time, voice, and self is visibly performed in the visual presentation of the work on the page. Yet it is the space between each prose vignette, each intricately imagined possible world, that allows us to see the work's myriad potentialities, selves, and fictive topographies in sharper relief. As Stonecipher herself observes, "as soon as the man came around the café in the evening shilling newspapers, then we remembered that our little world was only one of a profusion of worlds—a single bubble clinging to the great foam" (62).

⁂

Kaminsky's *Deaf Republic*, like Stonecipher's *Transaction Histories*, engages white space, silence, and rupture as stylistic devices and extended metaphor. Presented as a dramatic play-in-verse, the stunning poems in this volume frequently end not with a final line, but instead with dictionary entries, translating spoken words into a sign language devised by the speakers of the poems themselves. In such a way, the poems transcend speech, just as Stonecipher's prose paragraphs embrace elision and rupture if only for possibility to accumulate within their luminous architectures. Similarly, throughout *Deaf Republic*, silence comes to signify not only secrecy, but agency, hope, and resistance.

"You are alive," Kaminsky writes, "therefore something in you listens" (13). This rapt attentiveness is revealed as the most easily forgotten lesson of poetry in a postmodern political landscape. Fittingly, the dramatic verse of *Deaf Republic* actively involves the reader in this reframing of listening as prayer, as invocation, revolution, and inevitable transformation. He writes, for example, in "Deafness, an Insurgency, Begins,"

> Our hearing doesn't weaken, but something silent in us strengthens.
> After curfew, families of the arrested hang homemade puppets out of their windows. The streets empty but for the squeaks of strings and the *tap, tap,* against the buildings, of wooden fists and feet.
>
> In the ears of the town, snow falls. (14)

Here Kaminsky uses caesura and careful pacing to evoke the concept described by Miller, of time as chronology, a beginning collapsed into an end. As this piece unfolds, the end-stopped stanzas become charged with tension, as though each rupture signifies both the accumulation of history and its eventual undoing. Within the world of these poems, silence becomes both a foreshadowing and an appeal, as these gaps leave room for the reader to participate in the poems' revolutionary politics.

Like Stonecipher's *Transaction Histories*, *Deaf Republic* reframes silence as possibility, as loss and its inevitable transformation. As Kaminsky himself observes, "silence moves us to speak" (29).

"My Heart Was Clean"
On the Politically Charged Work of Silence in Poetry

IN *THE METAPHYSICS OF YOUTH*, Walter Benjamin observes that "[c]onversation strives toward silence, and the listener is really the silent partner. The speaker receives meaning from him; the silent one is the unappropriated source of meaning" (6). In other words, it is the space between words that sets off language, the dim background against which a light becomes visible. For Benjamin, silence was the precondition for a community out of which story arises, and the vast expanse waiting just beyond its inevitable end.

Three collections of poetry fully do justice to this complex relationship between silence, narrative, and the tacit relationships out of which language is born. Julie Marie Wade's *When I Was Straight*, Eileen G'Sell's *Life After Rugby*, and Rajiv Mohabir's *The Taxidermist's Cut* each consider, albeit from vastly different conceptual vantage points, the ways silence makes possible our experience of beauty, which G'Sell describes as the "gift of dark lace." Indeed, this "dark lace" is woven into each poem in these finely crafted collections. For G'Sell, Mohabir, and Wade, the possibility of transcendence resides in the space between things, and it is always a bright aperture that gives rise to what Mohabir calls a "queer flutter that knocks about your ribs." These three books share an investment in allowing opulence to be complemented by the reader's own unspoken imaginative work and contemplation, offering us only G'Sell's "sound of boots through snow and the dark."

What's more, these writers show us a full range of approaches to the work that silence can do. In G'Sell's dense, image-driven lyrics, this purposeful withholding often takes the form of absent narrative scaffolding. "Arias" and "attics" exist in close proximity, yet we are never told how these relation-ships came to be. What is left unsaid becomes an invitation to the reader, a pathway into the book's rich fictive terrain. For Mohabir and Wade, however, each aperture manifests as a kind of rupture, a subtle violence done to voice and language. As Mohabir himself tells us, "Every time you speak they hear a different hell" (25).

⁂

In *Life After Rugby*, each line is gratifyingly dense in its presentation of images, types of rhetoric, and its vibrant soundscapes. For G'Sell, this dis-concerting proximity—of images, of lexicons, and of narratives—gives rise to countless elisions, as the relationships, the rules that govern this imagina-tive topography, are often left to the reader's imagination. We are offered "a cheekbone shyly brushing your wrist," though the speakers of these poems rarely tell us to whom a body, or an encounter, belongs.

In many ways, silence is intricately linked to pacing in this work, as the speed with which we transition does not afford time or space for exposition. It is the breathlessness of each poem, their restless movement and their dense, complex music, that allows silence to inhabit them so fully. After all, the relationships, the associations, and the resonances are too numerous to count. Reminiscent of Joshua Clover's *The Totality for Kids* and Kathleen Peirce's *The Ardors*, G'Sell's poems also fearlessly confront—through their satisfyingly dense constructions and their quick, unpredictable leaps—our own discomfort with silence, while at the same time, gesturing at its inev-itability. G'Sell elaborates,

> With the best of her Sugar Ray Leonard bob,
> She weaved beyond traffic.
>
> Symphony, prosperity, the loose mares of time.
> Homily of hominy, the long dreams and lime.
> Outside her glowing loungecar, igloos in space.

In many ways, these lines might be read as an ars poetica, as G'Sell ges-tures as the work's own "symphony" of disparate images, lexicons, and miniature soundscapes. In passages like this one, the reader begins to see that the poems are constructed against silence—as the speaker fills the air with her "Sugar Ray Leonard" and nonsensical rhymes—but also that the poems exist because of that negative space, as it is the absence of narrative scaffolding, and all that is left unsaid, that allows the story to grow wilder.

⚜

Mohabir's poetry reads as a novel variation on G'Sell's exploration of silence, elision, and readerly unease. While formally diverse, spanning tercets, couplets, and hybrid experiments, *The Taxidermist's Cut* is gracefully unified by an exploration of silence as a kind of violence, a rupture in the faultlessly woven tapestry of voice, narrative, and community. Mohabir writes, "Knowledge / of Violence: // where welts rose on my legs / from the riding crop hidden / by your headboard / the crumble of song / shuddered in my hands" (77). Here lineation, and its ensuing pauses, exist in tension with the sentence, as well as the syntactic unit. Clauses (like "knowledge of violence" and "hidden by your headboard") are halved by Mohabir's deft and provocative lineation. When read through the lens of the book's exploration of cultural otherness, these stylistic gestures take on a new and conceptually arresting significance, as Mohabir shows us that silence—in poetry, in culture, and in our own consciousness—is politically charged.

Through his accomplished craft and thoughtful approach to style, Mohabir shows us the myriad ways that censorship—and that fear—deeply rooted in our culture, of confronting difficult questions—is gradually internalized, shaping our conscious experience even in solitude. This, Mohabir shows us, is the ultimate form of violence and intrusion. He elaborates,

> Your parents are at Bible study, leaving you alone with the devil inside.
> Your clothes are strewn about the floor.
>
>
> The rain ricochets drops through the windowpane.
>
> Your drops drone and soar from the opened window as cicadas.
>
> Inside you rain. You are a forgery. Not a wolf. Not an Indian. Not a son.
> (30)

What is particularly revealing in this passage is Mohabir's adept and skill-ful use of caesura. Here, the work's meaningfully timed pauses, the persistent stop and start, give rise to an uneasy, hesitant music (most visible in phrases like "…as cicadas. / Inside you rain."). We are shown that the voice of culture (which manifests powerfully in lines like "You are a forgery") ultimately engenders silence, even in the speaker's uncontested solitude. Yet at the same time, Mohabir calls our attention to the music that silence allows us to hear. What's more, he reminds us of the persistence of voice, and of music, even as the voice of the establishment drones through "the opened window" (30).

⁂

Like Mohabir and G'Sell, Wade's poetry exists at the interstices of speech, silence, and unease. Presented as a book-length exploration of the speaker's life before she came out as a lesbian, the poems in this stunning collection are haunted by a kind of shadow story, a narrative that resides just beneath the surface of these lively, jocular poems. Like G'Sell's poetry, these pieces exist against silence, and the confrontation—with selfhood, identity, and desire—that inevitably ensues.

As the book unfolds, each poem becomes a poignant dramatization of what's left unsaid. Yet at the same time, speech calls attention to its own artifice, as Wade's poems are constantly gesturing—at turns playfully, knowingly, and sorrowfully—toward all that cannot, will not, be spoken aloud. Wade writes, "I could tell my mother how / I wanted her to brush my hair / & braid it with ribbons / / I could tell my father how / I loved baking cookies & / pinning damp clothes on the line" (18). Here what's perhaps most reveal-ing is the line break and ensuing pause before "pinning damp clothes on the line." The moments of elision, as in Mohabir's work, become politically charged, as Wade's speaker struggles to signify and perform an identity that is foreign to her. Through her silence, the speaker also experiences herself as foreign, and this, for Wade, becomes the ultimate form of violence.

Yet she also shows us silence as agency, as manipulation of a cultural system, as well as readerly expectations. "I might have smiled more then," Wade writes, "the part of my lips so often mistaken / for happiness. In fact, it was something else— / a fissure, a break in the line—the way / a paragraph will sometimes falter / until you recognize its promise as / a poem" (6). In much the same way that Wade's speaker masquerades in her interactions with others, the moments of rupture and elision within the poem ultimately toy with the reader's preconceived ideas about how a narrative should or ought to unfold. Here the pause, that subtle and playful rupture before "a poem," the subsequent delay before narrative resolution, exemplifies the ways silence in Wade's work gives rise to suspense, surprise, and wonder.

That speechlessness engendered by culture is appropriated and recontextualized in a way that empowers the speaker, rather than censoring her. Like Mohabir and G'Sell, Wade shows us that each moment of elision contains multitudes within it. It is in these liminal spaces—the glowing aperture, the tentative sigh, the pause for breath—that the rules of language no longer hold, and anything becomes possible.

"Let Her Balance on Nothing"
Notes on Victimization, Complicity, and the Gaze

MARIA LUGONES OBSERVES that "through traveling to other people's 'worlds' we discover there are 'worlds' in which those who are the victims of arrogant perception are really subjects, lively beings, constructors of vision even though in the mainstream construction they are animated only by the arrogant perceiver and are pliable, foldable, file-awayable, classifiable"(4). Lugones rightly calls attention to the ways persuasive rhetoric often forecloses the possibility of empathy, reducing the humanity of its subjects to signification, that simple equivalence that fits neatly within a reductive explanation of the world around us. For Lugones, it is a kind of arrogance to believe that the complexities of inner experience can be fully captured, and faithfully rendered, by the limited repertoire of formal argumentation.

Two poetry collections engage these complex questions of rhetoric, victimization, and complicity. Gillian Cummings's *The Owl Was a Baker's Daughter* and Jennifer Minniti-Shippey's *After the Tour* consider, and thoughtfully critique, the implicit arrogance of any master narrative. Though vastly different in form and thematic approach, these two carefully crafted volumes share an investment in unearthing, and revising, the politics and power structures enacted in language, perception, and meaning-making. As each book unfolds, we are shown both the necessity of, and the limitations inherent within, the strict conventions of narrative. For Minniti-Shippey and Cummings, stylistic innovation—whether in the form of fragmentation, hybridity, collage, or the most cinematic of montages—offers the possibility of a story that does not offer a teleological end, and a more ethical way of documenting the difficult, complex cultural moment we inhabit.

This connection between formal innovation and ethics comes through most visibly in these writers' use of silence, white space, and rupture. It is in these bright apertures that Cummings and Minniti-Shippey invite uncertainty, ambiguity, and complexity back into the act of storytelling. In a culture that privileges speech over silence, Cummings and Minniti-Shippey are brave enough to leave some things unsaid. In doing so, these innovative practitioners create a ledger of history, perception, and suffering that does not serve a teleological end, instead engaging the discontinuous, discrete, and often contradictory nature of sensory experience.

⁂

Cummings's *The Owl Was a Baker's Daughter* takes Shakespeare's Ophelia and her voicelessness as its artistic subject. Presented as a book-length sequence of linked persona pieces, the poems in this stunning volume consider the ways we as a culture are disoriented by silence, trained from the very outset to fill the gaps, fissures, and elisions that manifest in language. In this way, Ophelia's voicelessness becomes an alluringly absent center around which Cummings's text orbits. Though archival in its genesis, *The Owl Was a Baker's Daughter* proves thoroughly modern in its presentation, and interrogation, of language, gender, and silence.

What's perhaps most striking about Cummings's approach is the way that she acknowledges, and moves beyond, complicity in a broken cultural mechanism. Because the poems themselves are persona-driven, an attempt to imagine that dress, that body "lingering in the swirl" of dark water (3). In such a way, Cummings recognizes, and fully owns, the undeniable impulse to create meaning from a world that is "fleeting" and illusory, "like a railroad's wish to lead nowhere" (6). Yet she proffers the bright apertures, the space between one dream and the next, as an alternative to the all-too-familiar master narrative, that story "taut in / gnarl and gold" (42). She writes, for example, in the opening poem,

> Meanwhile, she wants to die and does
> not know: to the body and its burden
> or to the self that pretends to be body.
> She steps and one thousand moths lift,
> lift lightly, spiral-whirl. They flicker and fleck,
> weaving a world around her […] (3)

Here Cummings offers a provocative metaphor for her own practice. Just as "one thousand moths lift," "weaving a world around" Ophelia, the poems themselves orbit around her silence, as a rich and complex linguistic tapestry arises out of her speechlessness. Yet the poems are gorgeously fractured in narrative, in syntax, and in their semantic meaning, fully acknowledging their debt to Shakespeare's heroine, her voice "blasted with ecstasy."[4]

Approached with that in mind, Cummings offers a vision of the classic narrative arc that carves space for the other to speak, whether or not she avails herself of that invitation. That fissure, that elision becomes a home, appropriately liminal, for possibility to reside in. It is in these gaps that Cummings's gorgeously fractured narrative courts expansion, response, and proliferation, welcoming the destabilizing impulses of her audience.

As Cummings herself writes, *"Go. Home. To the silence"* (33).

❧

Like Cummings's collection, Minniti-Shippey's *After the Tour* considers the ways rhetoric and teleology silence the other, but also engages the possibilities inherent in that silence. Constructed as a book-length sequence of lyric pieces, which at turns address soldiers, friends, lovers, and selection committees, Minniti-Shippey's poems traffic in uncertainty, proffering alternatives to the familiar narratives that circulate within our culture. Perhaps most striking is a sequence of poems addressed to a young soldier, "at twenty a man," as he is deployed and as he gives thanks for "three weeks with no fire" (9).

By delving into the minds and hearts of those individuals our culture frequently speaks for, Minniti-Shippey creates a poetics of empathy and resistance, challenging the belief that storytelling is one more "thing to master" (19). I find Minniti-Shippey's questioning of our traditional models of reading and writing—in which the construction of knowledge is framed as a visible wielding of mastery—to be compelling and heartening in its ethical sensibility. Like Cummings's presentation of Ophelia, Minniti-Shippey's lyric strophes revel in the space between perspectives and worldviews, finding beauty and redemption in ethically fraught territory—the thematic terrain that other less skilled writers would shy away from.

She writes, for instance, in "To the Boy Reading *Harry Potter* on His Bunk in Afghanistan,"

> …Your brothers play
> card games out of bright-hot boredom.
> Some you love return—you'll greet them
>
> with a fist to solar plexus, generous
> sweep of boot to shin. Blood out,
> blood in. It's a kind of wisdom. (9)

What's revealing here is that Minniti-Shippey recognizes the young soldier not solely as perpetrator, but as a victim caught in a broken cultural machine. From a stylistic standpoint, the poem makes intriguing use of enjambment as the lineation, and the seemingly orderly structure of the poem, becomes a form of violence done to voice and narrative. Yet as the lines visibly rupture the speaker's voice, Minniti-Shippey calls attention to the implicit cruelty of the master narrative, and the incongruities of the artificial order we tend to impose upon unruly sensory experiences.

For Cummings and Minniti-Shippey, it is in disorder, rupture, and chaos, that the possibility of complexity resides. And they show us, fracture by fracture, one elision at a time, that these gorgeously fragmented structures, charged with tension, offer a representation of human experience that is more real, more just, and more true. As Minniti-Shippey herself reminds us, "*the heart, from its great distance, watches*" (55).

The Experimental Feminist Text as Event

The Page as a Visual Field

Asiya Wadud, Gracie Leavitt, & Eve L. Ewing

IN AN ISSUE of *The American Poetry Review*, Carol Ann Johnston notes that "The early avant-garde's play with poetic language as visual art grasped the change in poetic emphasis from aural to visual [...] The influence of Cubism and Dadaism encouraged poets to see the page as verbal collage" (45–46). Johnston rightly calls attention the transformative work of poets like Stéphane Mallarmé and William Carlos Williams, whose writing questioned—and substantively revised—prevailing ideas about aesthetic pleasure. Yet the seismic shift that Johnston describes encompassed not just writing, but also the book as a physical object. Texts like "A Throw of the Dice," "The Corset," and *Spring and All* questioned our most basic assumptions about typesetting, white space, and the boundaries of the printed page as a unit of meaning.

Three contemporary poets build on the early avant-garde's experimentation with the page as a visual field, offering us collections that expand our sense of what is possible within a bound and printed book. Gracie Leavitt's *Livingry*, Asiya Wadud's *Crosslight for Youngbird*, and Eve L. Ewing's *Electric Arches* share a commitment to language that performs its meaning across the vast expanse of the page. In many ways, these writers' highly performative language calls attention to its own containment—by grammar, by genre conventions, and by the preconceived ideas that readers bring to the book as a cultural artifact. Ewing, Wadud, and Leavitt make visible, through their innovative artistic practice, this containment of voices and texts.

❧

As each collection unfolds, we are offered language that breaks boundaries—between the written and the visual arts, between representation and metaphor, between types of aesthetic experience—rendering us suddenly aware of the limitations we impose upon language before it has even begun to unfold before us. For some readers, this presentation of language might be jarring, even irreverent, as we are not used to texts that make their own rules. However, as Ewing herself reminds us, "The space was always there" (45).

❧

Leavitt's *Livingry* often reads as an exercise in scale. Here, we are offered poems that are slim and tersely lineated, white space overwhelming the texts' seeming smallness. Yet the language in *Livingry* resists this categorization, reacting against any possible description of the writing as diminutive, orderly, or neat. Leavitt invokes textual difficulty as an aesthetic gesture, and the careful withholding of meaning becomes a purposeful part of the reader's experience. In this way, the interplay of the poems' visual appearance and their metaphorical richness, and their relative scale in relation to both the page and the work that's asked of the reader, creates a provocative tension, a spark that ignites the collection.

The poems themselves read as dense soundscapes, as Leavitt eschews the semantic meaning of words in favor of their sonic richness. Reminiscent of Zukofsky's sound-based translations, the poems in *Livingry* challenge our limiting definitions of meaning and coherence, envisioning the poem as a space in which to offer alternative frameworks for thinking, storytelling, and elegizing. She writes, for example, in "Loose Leaf,"

> This morning
> the mystery
> shattered itself, but I
> don't want to
> only ornamentally
> absorb, therein
> sly call perhaps
> to be a part and
> separate...(4)

Here Leavitt offers lines that are as charged as they are minimalistic. Though parsed out two or three words at a time, the language in this sonically vibrant, singing poem overwhelms the seemingly small rhetorical space in which it is housed. What's more, as Leavitt transitions from "morning" to "mystery," from ornaments to their inevitable shattering, it is the moments of rupture, the pauses between each measured line, that set off each line's intricate and tangled music. For Leavitt, "to be a part and / separate" is a necessary part of the poem's work, a metaphor for lineation as much as it is for the poem's appearance on the printed page. Leavitt reminds us, subtly and skillfully, that poems are visual compositions, even—or especially—when we fail to realize it.

***

Electric Arches expands on Leavitt's consideration of poetry as an inherently visual endeavor. Filled with original artwork, handwritten notes, and poems on black pages, Ewing's poems challenge our culture's fixation on book publication as a way of claiming authority within a linguistic landscape that is inherently unstable. What's striking about Ewing's work is the way she embraces this uncertainty.

Ewing destabilizes, through her provocative visual experimentation, our idea of the book object as finished, static, and not subject to change. By transitioning from typewritten text to handwritten notes and drawings, Ewing questions the way our culture elevates the finished product, while devaluing the processual. Ewing places seemingly impromptu notes squarely within a perfect-bound book, carving a space for experimentation, improvisation, and play within a form heretofore reserved for language functioning as product and commodity. Ewing writes, for example, in "the first time [a re-telling],"

> This time she screamed at me. 'You little nigger! You almost hit me with that bike! Go back to your nigger Jesse Jackson neighborhood!' I told my mom and she *told me the flying bike should only be for weekends, but okay, I could use it just this once.* (8)

It is important to note that the second half of this passage is handwritten, beginning with "told me the flying bike…" (8). For Ewing, breaking free of cultural stereotypes requires re-envisioning the forms of discourse that bear oppression into the world, that give injustice its form and structure. She boldly weaves the language of oppression, unredacted racial slur and all, into this revolutionary text, confronting individual and shared trauma in order to move beyond it. The transition to handwritten notes, then, becomes politically charged, as Ewing gestures at a version of personal and shared history that could be opened to substantive change, strikethroughs, and revisions.

What's more, Ewing reveals the book object, and the textual economies in which it circulates, as being bound up in existing mechanisms of power in our culture. She provocatively challenges the ways we assign value to language, as we tend to revere finished, typeset, bound product over the artifact of its process. For Ewing, process is where the possibility lies, since in this liminal space, the rules with which we are familiar no longer hold.

Wadud's *Crosslight for Youngbird* blends the hybrid forms with documentary poetics and the lyric essay. Like Leavitt and Ewing, Wadud calls our attention to the preconceived ideas we bring to the book as a cultural artifact, and the assumptions we make about language before it has even begun to unfold before us. *Crosslight for Youngbird* takes as one of its primary considerations the arbitrary categories we impose upon types of writing, distinctions that are actually more fluid than we tend to acknowledge. Wadud shows us that it is hybridity that creates a more complete account of shared experience, an artifact of cultural memory that is more just and more true.

Like Leavitt and Ewing, Wadud summons the reader's preconceived ideas about form and genre by attending to the work's appearance on the page. In "home 16 ways," for example, the pristine prose paragraphs create a semblance of order, and artificial sense of unity, which the language itself interrogates and unravels. We encounter "a younbird" and its "able wings" alongside "bismillah calca" that "makes da bone firm" (3). The reader is rendered suddenly and startlingly aware of the expectations they likely bring to prose—that the text will be consistent in the texture of its language, that it will be uniformly accessible and transparent in its meaning. Wadud provocatively writes against these readerly expectations of form and genre.

Here, her audience is rendered, at turns, confidante and linguistic other, as the text is at certain moments suddenly inaccessible. By rendering us aware of the limitations that we impose upon prose, if only by looking at it on the page, Wadud ultimately works to foster more open-minded reading practices. For Wadud, seeing the limitations we place on language, and seeing the ways a containment of voice is gradually internalized, is the first step toward change. And for Wadud, change begins in language, as this is the very foundation of the social order.

She writes, for example, in "Calais, onward,"

> empire wrought boundless
> mollusked isle full of light
> moored light come light
> a sepulcher if not
> mark a journey supplicate
> pray mohammed
> and Fatima
> pray amira (16)

Here Wadud creates a sense of "boundlessness" within the language of empire, ultimately working to expand what is possible within it. Like Leavitt and Ewing, Wadud uses the page as a visual field, creating a semblance of order and unity if only to call attention to their inherent artifice.

Wadud, Leavitt, and Ewing build on a Modernist inheritance of visual experimentation in poetry, ultimately using collage, hybridity, and performative language to challenge the limitations the readers impose upon their own voices. In doing so, these writers offer an expansive aesthetic, a poetics of inclusion and dialogue. By allowing many types of aesthetic experience and meaning-making to exist together in the same rhetorical space, they ultimately expand the boundaries of the book as a cultural artifact, allowing it to hold a shared history that is more just, more luminous, and more complete.

Modernism & the Question of Genre
On Julie Carr's *REAL LIFE: an Installation*

ANITA HELLE ARGUES in *The Structure of Obscurity* that Gertrude Stein's stylistic experimentation could be read as an attempt to transpose the techniques of other artistic mediums into the realm of poetry. We see Picasso's influence as she calls attention to the materiality of the medium, privileging the sonic qualities of language over its semantic meaning, and we glimpse the specter of a film reel in her unyielding repetitions. This particular variety of hybridity remained commonplace among Modernist creative practitioners, many of whom worked across artistic mediums.

In recent years, readers have seen a veritable renaissance of poetry that engages painting, sculpture, film, and photography. Yet most of this writing functions as ekphrasis in the most traditional sense. We are offered poems that reflect on artworks, yet fail to engage the technical repertoire of any medium other than their own. Julie Carr's *REAL LIFE: An Installation* stands apart from these more traditional ekphrastic projects. Unlike many of her contemporaries, Carr frames language as "a performance," rather than that familiar "narrative of striving." Presented as a series of discrete episodes, which range from "fourteen-line poems," "short prose pieces," and found language to performance scripts, Carr's text skillfully adapts the immersive and disjunctive gestures of installation projects to the literary arts. In this way, she breathes life into a Modernist inheritance that has been obfuscated by our culture's predilection for a clear narrative.

According to the Tate Museum's website, installation art functions as "large-scale, mixed-media constructions, often designed for a specific place or for a temporary period of time." This impulse toward ephemerality, and toward process, rather than product/commodity, is enacted in Carr's swift transitions between scenes, lexicons, and narratives. "Try breathing faster," Carr tells us as the text glides from "the sun" to a "hostile hostel" to "enormous projections of the inside of your own body" (123). Here the space between things becomes charged and complex, much like the fissures between a "beautiful emerald circular button" and "a grain of rice" in a work of collage or assemblage (139). As we shift between scenes and vantage points—whether we're made to see through the eyes of "the witch," "an absent mother," or "an old man"—we often glimpse the same bleak cultural landscape. These silences as we "jump across" these liminal textual spaces take on the significance of elegy, a collective mourning of a "the city as it once was" (187).

As her work engages the current political situation, Carr makes disconcerting, provocative, and effective use of statistics. The hybridity of an installation project, which often includes video, photography, sculpture, and painting, comes through in this project's genre hybridity. The repertoire of journalism is put to work as a way of contextualizing, and generalizing from, the poetic image. This innovative approach allows Carr to glide between objective and subjective ways of understanding the world. She writes, for instance, in "Into It 3,"

> Girl in office crying because she has had a miscarriage.
> Girl in office crying because she does not know grammar, never learned grammar, is graduating in one year without knowing what a sentence is.
> %
> Also, 23,000 homeless students in Colorado at this time. (36)

Here Carr suggests, through provocative juxtapositions, that the "girl in the office crying" is symptomatic of a broken social system. Her pairing of general language (i.e., "girl") with deeply personal narrative implies that the trauma is larger in scale, that this anonymous "girl" is an archetype within a bleak cultural topography. As Carr shifts to statistics in the final stanza of the quoted passage, the scale shifts once again, gesturing at the magnitude and scope of what is being mourned.

What's more, this passage underscores one of the work's central questions: What form does an elegy take, one that encompasses all that we have lost as a culture, as a nation, and as an artistic community? The work's hybridity and its adaptation of not one, but many, other mediums speak to the seemingly insurmountable task of elegizing what "real life" has become. In a piece called "Shakespeare's Rapes," Carr elaborates, "Men rape women all the time, said my 12-year-old daughter. When the book goes, 'they beat her up,' it means they raped her, it just didn't want to say it, she says" (70). The leap we are asked to make between the title and the piece's thoroughly contemporary subject matter speaks to the too-slow pace of real, palpable social change. In this way, the work's swift transitions between vantage points, places, and historical milieux suggest some degree of similarity among the various scenes and characters, all of whom struggle to change a larger cultural mechanism from within its confines.

With that in mind, we might read Carr's Steinian adaptation of the installation form as a kind of closed textual system, an experience that is at once immersive and self-contained. "I enter into this circulatory system," Carr tells us, only to discover that "the goal of our...system is the unhappiness of society" (31). The work takes on a well-executed circular quality, as we return again and again to the same child, "pretty in a haircut," who may or may not know she is wholly entrapped in a destructive culture's orbits (124). Carr writes,

> Jerry gets his cut short and Lulu gets hers cut shorter. They watch in the mirrors as their hair falls to the floor. Suddenly, inside the mirror, the face of a very, very old woman. Dull yellow eyes. Sharp teeth in a gaping mouth.
> She stares hard at Lulu as they walk out the door— (14)

What's revealing about this passage is Carr's conflating the quotidian with the grotesque, the uncanny, and the unspeakable. The absence of exposition, as we are presented with image after image, speaks to the ways in which even the most frightening possibilities have been normalized within a "system" that generates unhappiness. With remarkable skill and compassion, Carr has created an installation that holds a mirror to this culture, and its apparatus for generating, again and again, that "sorrowful laughter," the sound of "a world shifting away" (150).

The Poetics of Ephemera

Kate Greenstreet, Karla Kelsey, & Sarah Ann Winn

IN "EPHEMERA: A Manifesto," Sophia Terazawa poses the question, "Written word or strike out, WHAT comes first?" In many ways, she prompts us to consider the writing process as a series of redactions, the allure of a text residing in all that cannot, and will not, be said. As readers, we try to grasp the narrative before it disappears again, to glimpse its arc before the light begins to fade. For Terazawa, it is this impermanence, and its ensuing silence, that allows the multitudes contained within a text, within a given story, and within the individual voice, to speak.

Three collections of hybrid work consider this complex relationship between voice, impermanence, and multiplicity. Kate Greenstreet's *The End of Something*, Sarah Ann Winn's *Alma Almanac*, and Karla Kelsey's *Of Sphere* consider narrative as a site of simultaneous gathering and unraveling, a tapestry that is unmade as quickly as it had appeared before us. Though vastly different in style and approach, these writers share an investment in framing silence, and absence construed more broadly, as revelation, a mirror held to both the story and its reader, reflecting back a "self flickering," all those "things the body wanted to say."

This desire to frame silence as revelatory, and to create a narrative that is "loose knit," comes through most visibly in these writers' use of white space. As each collection unfolds, it is the fissures, and the elisions that call meaning into question, that allow possibility to accumulate. Though taking many forms, ranging from text and image project to lyric essay, these three books present the gaps between words as both "wall" and "window," a "dark wondering" that equips the reader with "wings."

✦

Greenstreet's *The End of Something* begins its provocative elisions with the title, which refuses to name the lost object, setting the stage for an elegy that is ultimately unsayable. As the work unfolds, readers encounter a dreamscape comprised of both text and image, as photographs appear when we have reached the limit of what can be said in language. Throughout the work, silence takes hold when the unconscious begins its work in us, whether or not we fully understand its message or intent.

Greenstreet's speaker appears as a conduit, gripped by an alterity that speaks through her, a presence over which she can claim neither ownership nor control. As she writes, "I don't follow the news. I have to follow something else." In this sense, Greenstreet's work is reminiscent of Modernist poet H. D., who looked to the unconscious mind as both master and muse. And much like H. D.'s masterpiece Helen in Egypt, Greenstreet's textual landscape is filled with dreams, which refract, and intrude upon, waking life. "Sometimes I see him out there," her speaker explains, "Here's the girl he wants to meet." What's striking here is the presentation of the speaker as outsider, othered within the terrain of her own psyche. In *The End of Something*, even the dreamscape is made strange again, a constant source of surprise and wonder.

Within the dream, as envisioned by Greenstreet, silence functions as both violence and a generative force, an inevitable "movement toward something." She writes, for instance, in "The Little Ghost,"

> She's like I used to be,
> so quiet and good.

She waits for me.
She wants to tell me things.

Greenstreet leaves the reader here to wonder what is about to be revealed, and what the speaker once was. Subtly and skillfully, she calls our attention to the narrative's elisions as a dismantling and a source of possibility, an invitation to the reader to build what has been taken down. By inviting the reader into the text, to collaborate, and to participate actively in the process of creating meaning, Greenstreet implicates her audience in this interrogation of the unconscious mind, its dream-logic, and its inevitable blurring of boundaries between the dream and waking life. Here, we see our own guilt, and our own wishes, reflected back at us. As Greenstreet herself observes, "what haunts are not the dead // but the gaps left in us by the secrets of others."

⁂

Karla Kelsey's *Of Sphere* continues this interrogation of the unconscious mind, and relatedly, the limits of language for rendering inner experience. Throughout the work, she reminds us of the logic and causal relationships embedded within seemingly innocuous grammatical structures. Like Greenstreet, Kelsey reminds us that dreams, visions, and the hidden mind often resist the constraints of language. Her project attempts to exist within the strictures of grammar, while at the same time, expanding what is possible within its implied logic. We see her opening door after door inside what we thought was a single room. Needless to say, the space between things accumulates. "Whereas the world begins in language, the dancer begins in silence," Kelsey reminds us (57).

Presented as a series of lyric essays, which occupy different realms ranging from "biosphere" to "atmosphere" and "hydrosphere," the hybrid texts in Kelsey's collection invoke the history of Western philosophy while challenging its implicit patriarchal logic. "I approach the text to learn whether or not I will be spared the headache, stomachache, shoulder wound," she writes (38). For Kelsey, logic has its limits and its duration, as the boundaries between self and world, between the conscious mind and all that has been buried beneath its surface, remain inherently unstable. For Kelsey, freedom exists in this uncertainty.

She elaborates,

> in answer to absence:
> gutting the animal of what makes it
> so beautiful
>
> remainder left to the field … (77)

Here Kelsey calls our attention to culture's discomfort with silence, elision, and rupture. Collectively, we long for the clear narrative, the graceful arc of story. As readers, our first impulse is to fill the gaps with language, to "answer" the "absence" that has been set before us. We are reminded, throughout *Of Sphere*, of what happens in the space between words, in that pause between one thought and the next. In these liminal places, these thresholds, the rules of language no longer hold. As Kelsey herself writes, "to cross [a] threshold" is to walk through the door and "into home" (77).

Sarah Ann Winn's *Alma Almanac* continues this exploration of silence, ephemerality, and dream-logic. Presented as a series of lyric pieces, which are interspersed with found forms, such as indices, appendices, and notes, the work in this collection leaps provocatively between various ways of seeing, and different ways of being in the world. We drift between narrative and its unraveling, story and its artifacts, that echo of what was been said before we walked into the room.

As the book unfolds, Winn calls our attention to what cannot, and will not, be said aloud. The "pamphlet lacks the last few pages, contains only suggestions for how to open a long-lost letter from your dead," Winn explains (38). For Winn, the unspeakable is housed in the body, its memory at once visceral and mysterious, a "storm" buried beneath the mind's glittering surface (36). The book may be read as an attempt to reconcile language with all that resists its strictures, a work that calls attention to its own impossibility, its ambition and boundless inquiry. "*I want to understand you,*" Winn writes, "which is to say / *I do not understand*" (33.)

In many ways, Winn's formal daring amplifies the book's mystery. Through the wonderful performative quality of each line, we are made to experience the speaker's discovery of language and its limits, as the fractured forms constantly gesture at what cannot be said, all that does not fit within their framework. Winn elaborates,

Fig. 1811: A marred fallen leaf, the spectrum of apple colors. The page where small jaws gnawed a name. (7)

Here Winn, subtly and skillfully, calls our attention to language as visceral and embodied, but also the vast terrain of bodily experience that does fit within the frameworks of language. Like Greenstreet and Kelsey, Winn calls our attention to all the realms of experience that are silenced by language, its rules and its implicit ordering of the world around us. In much the same way that "small jaws gnawed a name" on the page, Winn gives us language that aches with absence, these tacit exclusions and foreclosed possibilities.

If a poetics of ephemera is a simultaneous weaving and unraveling, Greenstreet, Kelsey, and Winn show us both the beauty and the danger inherent in this kind of impermanence. We are given silence as possibility, as space for the reader to speak, a terrain hospitable to echo, ambiguity, and multiplicity. Yet at the same time, these writers show us language and its implicit rules as redaction, as limitation and erasure. Thought vastly different in their respective relationships to form, Greenstreet, Kelsey, and Winn have ultimately taken linguistic constraint and reimagined it, transforming it from outright violence to a kind of generative destruction, a field on fire that makes way for the new.

The Violence of Collision
Notes on Collage, Precarity, and the Archive

IN A CO-AUTHORED essay on ephemera and ephemerality, which appeared in *Amodern 7*, Priti Joshi and Susan Zieger observe that "Ephemerality might be described as the lived condition of an industrial modernity, founded on disposability, fluctuating value, and illusion." It could also be said that the fleeting nature of so much material culture challenges our beliefs about history, as it undermines pretensions to enduring cultural relevance. The archive, however, offers an exception to this rule, a space removed from capitalist frameworks, where the remnants of disparate historical milieux may collide, challenge, and illuminate one another.

Three collections of poetry and hybrid work explore the unique potentialities of the archive, a liminal space that is inevitably charged with tension and possibility. Kathleen Peirce's *Vault: A Poem*, Mary-Kim Arnold's *Litany for the Long Moment*, and Amy Pence's *[It] Incandescent* utilize collage, assemblage, and juxtaposition to explore the precarity of our beliefs about history, its narratives, and its structures. While vastly different in form and approach, these three texts share an investment creating dialogue across cultures and historical moments. Even more importantly, they expertly reveal the violence inherent in this collision. As Mary-Kim Arnold notes, "[t]he life is there, encased in its own death. Its own catastrophe (57).

For these three prescient writers, the violence inherent in collage, assemblage, and artistic collision is as inevitable as it is generative. Scholar and poet Myung Mi Kim has long noted the violence of the experiment, in which boundaries, traditions, and readerly expectations are destroyed in order to make way for something new. In *[It] Incandescent*, Amy Pence attributes this generative violence to history itself and the artistic legacy she herself has inherited. She leaves us with the image of Emily Dickinson, "collecting her horrors—a box inside."

❦

Presented as a series of visual texts, Amy Pence's *[It] Incandescent* reads as an extended engagement with Emily Dickinson's poetry, one in which the adept placement of the words on the page heightens our experience of language. More often than not, we are unsure as readers whether to approach Pence's text as homage or destruction, a dismantling of tradition in order to create a bright aperture, that opening that beckons "through the sun-stilled trees."

In many ways, the destructive impulse inherent in Pence's poetics is ideally suited to the book's narrative arc. She explores, through fragmentation, ellipsis, and linguistic collage, the trauma housed within—and often buried inside—the archive, that "box of phantoms" that must, at some point, be opened. She writes, for example, midway through the collection:

> *It:* that Memory you have to step around, upon. *It*, unnamed and unpersoned, made the *It* in Emily go to her knees—

> At what cost our denial? How we go to our knees.

Pence creates a poetics of trauma and redemption, an aesthetic predicated on building narrative, and discovering meaning, "by degrees." In doing so, Pence shows us that as T. S. Eliot later argues, quite famously, the past is contained within the present. Here, history and modernity are conflated in even the texture of the language itself. By pairing words like "opon" with more colloquial speech, Pence shows us that history, its trauma, its silences, and its elisions are embedded within the minutiae of syntax and grammar.

It is perhaps for this reason that collage and assemblage become a powerful form of resistance. It is the space between things that speaks most audibly, that gestures at the multitudes of what cannot, will not, be spoken aloud. "Above them, the Good Death / hovers," Pence writes, "that happen - / that gap / before the slaughter." Here fragmentation offers a meditation of the precarity of voice, as the threat of not only silence, but also self-censorship, looms large. Here the gaps, the ruptures, the elisions become performance, as Pence offers us language spectacularly aware of its own precarious labor.

✳

For Arnold, as in Pence's work, the precariousness of voice and narrative are tangible, embodied, viscerally felt. Presented as a book-length hybrid text, which meditates on the narrator's adoption from rural Korea and subsequent search for her biological family, *Litany for the Long Moment* offers a poignant and beautifully crafted meditation on linguistic displacement. Arnold calls our attention—in prose as subtle as it is evocative—to the physical difficulty of inhabiting a language that is foreign to our sensibilities. She shows us the myriad ways that personal identity is predicated on place, and the precarity of this necessary context. "I remain tethered to abstractions," Arnold tells us, "mother, motherland, mother tongue" (75).

As Arnold draws from the archival material surrounding her own childhood and family history, we are made to see—powerfully and indelibly—that the collision of languages, of cultures, of histories, often reveals their incommensurability. Arnold warns us, "Repeating a word loudly with more urgency will only get you so far" (19). What is perhaps most powerful about this book, though, is the way Arnold gestures at language as an embodied phenomenon. "I am struck by...the apparatus of language," Arnold notes, "and the physical difficulty of making sounds that are unfamiliar" (19). Throughout *Litany for the Long Moment*, the body seems to reject language that does not arise from its history, from the memories and narratives housed within its own walls.

Collage and assemblage offer a way of performing and dramatizing this alienation, as well as revealing the violence of imposing narrative in a strange language. We are made to see—through the fragments of a story that cannot, will not, be spoken—that there are some connections that narrative convention is ill-equipped to fully articulate. Arnold elaborates,

> Among the documents my mother kept are: several copies of a three-page "social study" of which I am the subject; a record of medical examinations, letters from the director of the orphanage where I lived for some time, and a few photographs of me: as a child in Korea, as I arrived in New York. (56)

Here the aperture—that luminous space between "records" and "photographs" within the archive—becomes a performance, calling our attention to the artifice inherent in any narrative scaffolding we attempt to impose. Indeed, absence and elision seem more real, more true. Arnold shows us that some meaning can only be grasped in this precarious linguistic context, as there is always the thing for which there is no word, the word "you may not yet know you want to say" (20).

⁂

Kathleen Peirce's *Vault: A Poem* continues this exploration of violence, the archive, and the unspeakable. Presented as an extended sequence, which takes the form of lineated verse, epigraphs, and lyric fragments, Peirce's work engages source texts dating from the Renaissance to the present moment, her poetry offering an interstitial space in which these disparate voices become a seamless chorus, gloriously unified in their lyricism. In many ways, Peirce's seamless integration of these many voices gestures at a kind of universality, the shared condition of being tethered to a language that does not fully do justice to inner experience.

In many ways, this gesture comes through most visibly in the moments between sections, where the reader is frequently asked to follow as we leap from one voice to another, one century to the next. Peirce reminds us that *after this* means *because of this*, yet at the same time, she approaches time as linear, recursive. As a result, our ideas about causation are destabilized through the work's provocative juxtapositions and associative leaps. She writes,

> *. . . Everything is broken.*
> *Reddish feathers growing at the joint, the pronged hand*
> *remind, supply.*

56.

> *swee swee swee the art, swee*
> *the art, sweetheart* (32)

Here Peirce reveals the archive as a place where the rules of logic and causation no longer hold. As we transition from the surreal dreamscape filled with "broken" objects and "Reddish feathers," we find our predilection for narrative causation challenged and interrogated. Like Arnold and Pence, she shows us that this interstitial space of the archive offers a testing ground for new ways of imagining language, grammar, and the structures of meaning-making. As in Arnold and Pence's work, there is violence inherent in this destruction of old models, but it is a kind of violence that makes even the most ordinary things "more wild, more violet" (51).

The Generative Violence of the Experiment

IN A LECTURE on innovative writing, Myung Mi Kim argued that any artistic experiment is inherently violent, as the artist is dismantling an inherited tradition in order to make way for the new. For many writers, innovation does contain destruction in its very definition. After all, the experimental text cannot exist in the same space as the conventions that restrict its meaning, stifle its performativity, and deny its legitimacy.

Three books remind us that an experiment, though challenging elements of a familiar literary heritage, does not have to sacrifice unity of voice and vision. Karla Kelsey's *Blood Feather*, Kenji C. Liu's *Monsters I Have Been*, and Grace Talusan's *The Body Papers* skillfully dismantle received forms to offer alternative ways of creating meaning and coherence from the disparate phenomena of human experience. Though vastly different in style and scope, these three innovative texts share a commitment to a unity of concept, presenting us with larger questions about the politics of language that ultimately guide and focus the generative violence of the experiment. In their hands, innovation becomes an exercise in precision, as well as a legitimate danger. As Liu writes, "The under state / swarms our / documents. Our / lungs."

Kenji Liu's poetry collection, *Monsters I Have Been*, opens with an articulation of the artistic goals and the parameters of an invented poetic form, "frankenpo." Liu elaborates in this formal definition: "to create a new poetic text by collecting, disaggregating, randomizing, rearranging, recombining, erasing, and reanimating one or more chosen bodies of text, for the purpose of divining or revealing new meanings often at odds with the original texts."

As the book unfolds, the constraints and freedoms of "frankenpo" serve to unify the book's wild flights of the imagination, as *Monsters I Have Been* reads as an extended exploration of the possibilities inherent in this specific literary form.

In many ways, it is the intense focus of Liu's experiment that brings his discoveries into sharp relief. Culling text from a variety of sources, which range from screenplays to *New York Times* articles, feminist theory, U.S. presidential executive orders, and more, Liu shows us the beauty and danger contained within the same turn of phrase, which can house both violence and redemption, light and unspeakable darkness. The poems in *Monsters I Have Been* elucidate the arbitrariness of the signifier, while at the same time calling our attention to the subject's remarkable agency with respect to language.

Liu writes, for example, in "Thus I Have Heard," "We are visas / in a national / drowning. / Each of us an executive / decision, pursuant to clay. / Each a subsection / of protocol / and yet." Here Liu reconfigures language from unspecified source texts, reminding us that intent not only shapes outcome with respect to the words we use, but also that intent can bring to light the beauty that resides just beneath the surface of a seemingly unremarkable text. For Liu, the same language can carry revelation and violence, enlightenment and oppression.

What's more, he shows us the myriad ways that language is illuminated by conversation, dialogue, and juxtaposition. In many ways, the personae contained within *Monsters I Have Been* are strengthened, and refined, by conversation, as proximity brings a single voice into clearer focus. He writes, for instance, in "As the light diminishes again," "To fit the average, we come / as animals, with a pocket map / of the sky and nothing under. // How the ragged hairpiece gapes / open and declares teeth." This poem utilizes found text from Judith Butler's theoretical writings as well as the Heart Sutra. Approached with that in mind, the poem becomes a space for dialogue in which one texture of language complicates, and calls into question, the other. As Liu himself asks, "What masks / What power"?

⁂

Much like Liu's book, Grace Talusan's memoir, *The Body Papers*, reveals (and renegotiates) the politics inherent in language. Yet Talusan takes this kind of experimentation in a new direction, pairing text with found images as she investigates the authority, reverence, and doubt that we invest in various types of cultural documents. The artifacts that inhabit *The Body Papers* range from canceled passports to immigration forms to family photographs. These politically charged and authoritative documents are positioned in service of personal narrative, a gesture that proves as innovative as it is subversive. The hierarchies that we impose upon types of language are provocatively reversed. Talusan summons the authority of official documents, journalistic photographs, and the various traces of governmental power to further a personal narrative of risk, family ties, and discovery.

Talusan's daring reversal of these power structures comes through perhaps most visibly in her depiction of the journey of her emigration to the United States from Manila with her parents and siblings. Describing the obstacles her parents encountered as they applied for citizenship, she writes, "I was terrified. I had never thought about how meaningful U.S. citizenship was until I was told I didn't have it. With a shuffle of papers, life as I knew it could be lost. I am still astounded by how meaningful these papers are, how they are pasted onto our bodies and determine where and how we can move through the world." This powerful narrative, in which the narrator realizes the precarity of what she had remembered as a joyful childhood, is spliced with images of a canceled Philippine passport and a character reference in support of an application for United States citizenship.

In many ways, the images included in *The Body Papers* complicate and enrich the narrative proper. By pairing this section with these specific documents, for example, Talusan evokes the stateless and liminal status of her younger self. Yet at the same time, she provocatively claims the authority and power of these documents for her own narrative, a reversal of the ways in which we often shape and reshape personal narrative in the service of government procedure.

This investment in revealing, and challenging, the authority placed in government documents serves as a unifying force in this gorgeously wide-ranging and capacious narrative. Talusan writes, for example: "Without physical proof, I started to question whether I had even written [the letters]— a psychological pattern that I think is intertwined with the immigrant experience." As this powerful memoir unfolds, however, Talusan challenges the artificial divide culture has created between objective and subjective types of language, laying claim to both in prose as deeply felt as it is precise and sharply focused.

Kelsey's *Blood Feather*, like the work of Liu and Talsuan, utilizes experimental language in service of social justice. This book-length poem, inspired by a rich store of archival material associated with women's history, manifests as three dramatic monologues spoken by different personae. The whole of the archive is subsumed into the voices of these richly imagined narrators, with Kelsey drawing from texts that range from Aristotle to Pina Bausch, Julian Beck, Richard Brody, Cheiro, and many other writers, philosophers, cinematographers, and thinkers. By challenging the fiction of the single speaker in such a way, Kelsey gestures at voice as a social construct, calling into question the myriad ways culture presupposes that ownership over language is even possible.

It is the unity of voice, remarkable given the scope and range of archival material represented in this volume, that renders Kesley's text as sharply focused as Talusan's narrative memoir and Liu's extended exploration of a single form. As the book unfolds, this unity of voice and vision is revealed as integral to the poem's deeply philosophical meaning. For Kelsey, the self, the single spoken voice, contains multitudes within it. She shows us, through her sharply focused experimentation, that the boundary between individual and community is porous and indistinct. She writes, for example, in *Blood Feather*:

> [...] the aesthetic problem of
> form exists essentially and simultaneously as
> a moral problem writes Deren in
> *An Anagram of Ideas on Art*
> and so how to perform an
> ethical relation to the footage of
>
> a flood mobile homes uprooted a
> man in a canoe paddling after
> his lowing cow the film then

cutting to the tremor of a
hand-held camera actress gagged and bound
to the bed how to punctuate

Here the speaker reflects on the ethical problems inherent in representation. If the boundary between self and other remains blurry, Kelsey asks us to consider where cultural appropriation begins when attempting to depict our own perceptions. In many ways, the philosophical quality of Kelsey's poetry is in itself subversive, as she uses the artistic repertoire of poetry to claim agency over a predominantly masculine philosophical tradition. In doing so, she reminds us that despite the rigid binary distinctions that circulate within culture, alterity inevitably resides within the subject, who is a world unto herself.

If innovation is in itself a destructive gesture, can that generative violence be placed in service of activism and advocacy through language? Kelsey, Talusan, and Liu show us that it is the precision of the experiment that constitutes its power. In each of these collections, this dismantling of convention is placed in service of a specific philosophical question. In other words, experimentation becomes an inquiry into the very specific rules associated with language. Here, language is wielded as veiled threat, as provocative reversal, as gloriously shattered syntactic convention. Yet it is this space between words that allows us to see the light.

"It Takes What Light It Wants"
Authority and Rebellion in Feminist Poetry

IN *PAPER MACHINE*, Jacques Derrida asserts that "I believe in the value of the book, which keeps something irreplaceable, and in the necessity of fighting to secure its respect" (28). Here Derrida frames the act of writing as both homage and destruction, a simultaneous dismantling and preservation of literary convention. After all, any creative practitioner chooses that element of tradition—what is truly "irreplaceable"—and bears it into the future, while discarding other aspects of their artistic inheritance. These choices, for many writers, are what instigates that "fight to secure respect," the recognition of the work as still being part of that lineage, in spite of the violence the author has done to it.

Three poetry collections by women fully interrogate the complex relationship between artistic tradition, perceived legitimacy, and rebellion. Anne Champion's *The Good Girl is Always a Ghost*, Carla Harryman's *Sue in Berlin*, and *Thicket* by Cate Peebles invoke familiar literary forms—namely couplets, tercets, and pristine prose paragraphs—only to reframe them as a vehicle for feminist critique. For Champion, Harryman, and Peebles, the strictures of form allow feminist creative practitioners to expand what is possible within their boundaries. Rather than discarding tradition altogether, these writers have chosen to summon the authority of an artistic lineage only to render their rebellion all the more formidable.

In many ways, this disruptive impulse is most visible in these writers' handling of the familiar. Because we are deceived by a text that looks like what we know, and appears legible on the page, we are willing to follow its author to the very periphery of what can be said in language. In such a way, an out-moded artistic repertoire is made to house truly provocative assertions about language, gender, and their relationship to the female body. As Champion herself notes, "The finest thing a woman can wear is her untethering" (64).

Champion's *The Good Girl is Always a Ghost* harnesses a vast range of forms—among them couplets, tercets, quatrains—from a mostly male liter-ary tradition. As the book unfolds, these vestiges of literary convention are brought to bear on the containment of women's voices, their bodies, and their sexuality. Presented as a series of persona poems in the voices of female historical figures, or epistles directly addressed to them, Champion's work is immediately reminiscent of Julianna Baggott's *Lizzie Borden In Love: Poems in Women's Voices* and Kara Candito's *Taste of Cherry*, among many other feminist texts.

The poems in Champion's collection span the full range of histories, regimes, and cultural milieux. The personae engaged include Marilyn Monroe, Eva Braun, Anne Frank, Rosa Parks, Judy Garland, Jackie Kennedy, and many more. Though thematically diverse, the work offered in this col-lection is unified by the friction that exists between form and content. Cham-pion calls our attention to the ways these women's voices resist the strictures of convention, and the language itself strikes sparks against its seemingly orderly presentation. She writes in "Eva Braun, Mistress to a Monster,"

> Politics, such things are men's concerns.
> The wolf loves me because I don't threaten
> authority. The wolf loves me painted pretty
>
> and demure—the weaker I am, the more
> he loves... (55)

Here Champion's lineation is especially telling. As she transitions from "I don't threaten" and "authority," the syntactic unit is literally halved, sug-gesting that the speaker does in fact maintain the potential to disrupt, to challenge, and do violence to the established order. The stanza break between "painted pretty" and the remainder of the clause ("and demure") suggests the speaker's hesitation, a bit of uncertainty and interior drama surrounding her traditional female role.

Though highly skilled with respect to her use of inherited forms, Champion often chooses the most poignant moments to break the patterns she's established with respect to lineation, the length of stanzas, and the breadth of her lines. She writes in "Eva Perón,"

> Don't ask me what they worshipped in this
>   disintegrating body, my heartbeat like skipping
>   stones across a lake. I used to love like a woman
>
>   famished, take men like a slingshot, like the bed
>   was nothing but a sky without a trace of storm. (61)

Here Champion's jagged margins evoke the speaker's own restlessness within her "disintegrating body," which the poem's neat tercets ultimately fail to contain. The book is filled with pieces like "Eva Perón," in which familiar forms are subtly varied, whether through the visual presentation of the work on the page, an irregular margin, or an abrupt end mid-couplet or mid-tercet. Champion writes in "Sally Ride Watches the Challenger Explode," as though reflecting on this repertoire of inherited form, "I can't understand this machine / of grief, its solitary gears, / its churning, its malfunctions" (42).

In *Thicket*, Peebles continues Champion's provocative meditation on the ways language and artistic convention work to contain women's voices. Indeed, Peebles explores the ways that inherited forms, and even grammar, lend an artificial sense of order to disruptive narratives and experiences. Presented as a series of short-lined poems and prose boxes with wide margins, Peebles ultimately uses these familiar forms to create a sense of claustrophobia on the part of the reader. In such a way, these seemingly innocuous couplets and prose boxes are made to house critiques—of their limitations, their arbitrary nature, and their implicit politics.

Peebles writes, for example, at the beginning of the collection,

> Before or after the great wind storm that winter
> when all the oaks at Versailles were ripped

by their hoary roots & thrown over the grounds
like mottled cadavers, before or after the century turned,

before we returned from abroad & moved forward...(4)

By setting the poem in Versailles, Peebles gestures at the unacknowledged privilege inherent in the artistic tradition she has inherited, and continues to inhabit, through her use of received forms. At the same time, the speaker's voice seems to resist the orderly structure of the poem's couplets as she recounts what are truly disruptive sensory experiences ("mottled cadavers" and the "hoary roots" of oaks, to name only a few discomfiting images). When considering the rhythms of the poem, the line seems to exist in tension with the syntactic unit, perhaps as a way of gesturing at the inherent artifice of the form, and the manner in which we attempt to give structure to an incongruous and unruly experience of the world around us.

As the work unfolds, the "thicket" emerges as a metaphor for language itself. The work's central question, then, revolves around the nature of change, and the creation of a more just structure for shared communications. In other words, is it possible to inhabit a forest, whether literal or conceptual, that is ultimately violent and threatening? Can we create something new there without tearing down what is old? As Peebles herself writes, "When the flood comes / we will be on our phones / searching for how / to save ourselves..." (42).

Peebles upholds the dialogue between tradition and innovation as a new frontier for many feminist practitioners desiring change. She writes near the end of the collection,

I don't know exactly
what real life is like: I know there are men posed,

contrapost, in perpetual reward; jars of dynasty's
hearts and spleens; all matter of admissions to

the netherworld—a body in a box & the box
in a box in a chest in the ground. (65)

Like Champion, Peebles remains skeptical of the neat "box in a box" that is our life in language, leveling these criticisms from within the most familiar of poetic structures. She gestures at the violence implicit in imposing an arbitrary structure on "real life," yet also the necessity of shared experience of language for creating a feminist consciousness.

Like Champion and Peebles, Harryman explores the relationship between language and gender, turning to invented and hybrid forms as a way of bridging the gap between tradition and innovation. Presented as a verse novel in discrete episodes, *Sue in Berlin* calls upon verse plays, lineated poetry, dramatic scripts, and the lyric essay to create a single narrative that is marked by provocative rupture and interruption. In such a way, Harryman offers a text that deceives at first with its familiarity, offering us language in a form we once thought we knew. Because Harryman begins with what is familiar, we are willing to follow her to the very periphery of what is legible in terms of form, grammar, and narrative.

Harryman writes in the opening lines of *Sue in Berlin*,

> From nowhere a distinguished looking
> Gentleman approaches our
> Band of withdrawn politicos.
> He's dressed in a pale suit
> His extended hand
> Lit by the moon glows
> Whitely
> And Sue disappears (11)

She begins with language as narrative as it is accessible. The philosopher Paul Ricœur once distinguished between symbolic language, which is language that generates meaning, and the language of signification. Here we are in the realm of signs, not yet in the work's richly imagined metaphorical terrain. This choice speaks to Harryman's carefully considered approach to experimentation, to entice the reader with what is familiar only to make them question every preconceived idea they may have about language, form, and what is possible within them.

Harryman writes in one of the book's final verse plays, "Anti-Masque,"

C2 (younger):   Heart in hand on wheel
                       Head on shoulder in window
                       Pale in winter with slow time
                       Tree in shadow by piano
                       Frequent a stirring a template
                       Model for me at breakfast…(100)

As we can see, Harryman's adherence to the conventions of grammar, syntax, and narrative early in the book opened up a space for her to experiment even more boldly in the work's later passages. Here, the poetic line replaces the sentence as the primary unit of meaning, each enjambment marking the beginning of a new vocabulary of imagery, a new metaphor, a new logic governing the language that unfolds before us. Like Champion and Peebles, Harryman works within the strictures of received forms only to expand what is possible within them. All that once was familiar to us becomes a vehicle for what is revolutionary. What's more, in all three collections, the authority of an inherited artistic tradition is summoned in service of "a single, throaty note," the call for a shared language that is more just and more true.

Unruly Language

Towards a Poetics of Disruption

Beyond Metaphor

On Prose by Chris Campanioni & Elizabeth A. I. Powell

IN *THE DIALOGIC IMAGINATION*, Mikhail Bakhtin observes that "the poetic symbol presupposes the unity of a voice with which it is identical, and presupposes that such a voice is completely alone within its own discourse" (328). For Bakhtin, one of the distinguishing features of poetic language is the use of the image to convey content that is narrative, emotional, or philosophical in nature. Even more importantly, the poetic image, in Bakhtin's estimation, arises out of the sonic and stylistic terrain the poet has created, responding to, and directly informing, the behavior of the language itself.

Two hybrid texts explore, and fully exploit, the possibilities that poetic language holds for innovative prose writing. Chris Campanioni's *the Internet is for real* and Elizabeth A. I. Powell's *Concerning the Holy Ghost's Interpretation of JCrew Catalogues* invoke recurring imagistic motifs as structural devices, the end result being a narrative arc that is not easily charted by familiar literary conventions. With that in mind, the image, for both of these prose writers, lends a sense of order to, and circumscribes the boundaries of, the imaginative terrain that these vibrant, complex characters traverse. Though vastly different in style and aesthetic approach, these innovative practitioners share an investment in expanding what is possible within the artistic repertoire of fiction, carving a space for lyricism, ambiguity, and experimentation within the familiar act of storytelling.

This destabilizing impulse is most visible in these writers' use of metaphor. As each book unfolds, metaphor is no longer mere adornment, a rhetorical flourish at the end of a lovely stanza. Instead, vehicle and tenor become organizing principles, offering a source of unity, and productive tension, within each novel's carefully considered meditation on the nature of representation. As Powell herself writes, "…until we can see clearly the way of the flower to the sun, we shall dwell in the photograph of the free world, forever and ever. Amen" (9).

⁂

Powell's *Concerning the Holy Ghost's Interpretation of JCrew Catalogues* takes as its artistic subject the incommensurability of reality and representation. To that end, the novel's central metaphor is that of religion, a comparison between the texts circulated within mass culture and the familiar holy books of the Christian church. For Powell, the mass-produced and mass-circulated image becomes almost divine for the constituents of a consumer society. As Powell observes, "the Holy Ghost moves words in the copywriter's mind as he sleeps in his room of burgundy velvet on the East Side of New York City" (9).

Throughout the book, this metaphor becomes a source of productive tension and complexity, particularly as Powell calls attention to a blurring of boundaries between secular and religious ways of thinking, perceiving, and being in the world. More specifically, Powell reminds us how religious frameworks for meaning-making subtly manifest in secular life, as they are so deeply ingrained in collective memory.

Powell writes, for example, early in the book,

> For blessed were Mindy's diet pills, for they helped to make her free. Blessed are too many diet pills when Mindy stood alone in memory; she therefore blacked out. But here captured on page twelve of the catalogue was the moment when Mindy was at the height of her speeded frenzy, meeting each click of the camera, each click of the speed in her brain with a facial expression so pure, so true, she sold a quarter-million of these dresses. (17)

Here Powell underscores the many ways mass culture equates weight loss with virtue, reminding us that asceticism began, after all, as a show of piety. What's perhaps most revealing about this passage is behavior of the language, as the work's central metaphor fittingly dictates tone, cadence, and diction.

In such a way, the lyricism of this invocation visibly enacts and performs the transformation of doctrine, as old forms are reconstituted with wildly unexpected and thoroughly modern content.

As Powell herself observes, "She believed in the holy American religion of the Self, although she had not thought it through too deeply" (119).

Like Powell's novel, Chris Campanioni's hybrid text, *the Internet is for real*, takes as its primary consideration the necessary tension between reality and representation. For Campanioni, this friction is amplified by technology, social media, and their undeniable presence within interpersonal relationships. The work's central metaphor, then, becomes the photographic image as signifier, rendering the physical body an "immaterial...daydream" and a deceptive chimera (237). As Campanioni himself asks in one of the book's more essayistic sections, "*The camera is us.* We have become so fully integrated into the machine as to become its greatest development: a living snapshot" (272).

If the boundary between reality and representation has been dismantled by the rise of readily accessible social networking, what does this mean for art? In Campanioni's estimation, the parameters of art are then expanded, as the most quotidian tasks become, at turns, performance and narrative, our being in the world a "visible plastic symbol," an adornment, and a satiric impulse (65).

Campanioni writes, for example, in one of the book's many discrete prose episodes,

> You make your way through a rave-like jungle as each crystal bulb pulses and changes color, swaying as though you *are* the jungle: a body forgotten or fused with an ecosystem or system of hardware. The self that has left its own skin. (32)

The word "system" here is telling, as Campanioni reminds us of our place in the various economies of language and representation that circulate around us. Social networks, then, become a kind of auction block, the subject's performance a commodity, its artifice intended to secure a place within this larger system of valuation. By describing the self as "a rave-like jungle," he posits the individual as a nexus for transpositions, transactions, and transformations when considering these larger systems of labor and value (32). However, Campanioni's work is most provocative in its considerations of deception in these technologized environments, in which the photographic image becomes a way of reclaiming power and agency within a broken cultural mechanism.

As Campanioni himself asks, "Send this message without subject or body?" (87).

If the act of representation is the most self-conscious of metaphors, then poetic language is a dramatization of the distance between the vehicle and its tenor. After all, there is no metaphor without some degree of separation, that bright aperture between language and its point of reference. Powell and Campanioni show us that in this gap, this fissure, transformation becomes possible. The ascent into the realm of the symbolic, that diction which generates possibility after possibility, becomes, for Powell and Campanioni, a way of destabilizing the familiar architecture of story. As Campanioni tells us, "Storyteller and stagehand; lyrical and expository, theoretical and autobiographical. I want to always be both" (114).

On Secrets, Light, & the Lyric Imagination
Henry Hoke, Kirsten Kaschock, & Matthew Rohrer

IN HIS ESSAY collection *Ozone Journal*, Peter Balakian defines *shadow* as a "force that follows something with fidelity" only to "cast a dark light" on that person, object, view, or perspective. For Balakian, this fraught proximity—a closeness that blocks the line of vision—is one of the most essential characteristics of a work of art. After all, it is what we sense, but do not yet see, that beckons us farther into a half-lit room. The careful architecture of a poem—a space that is gradually illuminated for the reader—depends upon all that is hidden as a necessary condition, much more so than the visible beauty or significance of a particular image.

Three hybrid works enact this intricate relationship between secrets, shadow, and the aesthetic imagination. In Henry Hoke's *Genevieves*, Kirsten Kaschock's *Confessional Sci-Fi: A Primer*, and Matthew Rohrer's *The Others*, the unknown emerges as a source of both light and its surrounding darkness. Though vastly different in style and approach, these writers share a gift for a skillful and calculated withholding, the suggestion of a buried narrative "quietly ghosting" all that is immediately perceptible. Here, what is hidden offers an invitation, an occasion for collaboration between the poem and its reader, creating a third space that belongs to both of them (and at the same time, neither of them). Each of these texts becomes "a glass bridge between buildings," the beginning of an incandescent structure that is built across temporal, psychic, and geographic boundaries.

Early in the twentieth century, modernists described this kind of innovative text as a "machine for generating meaning." The poet's task, then, was to guide the reader's imaginative work, slowly revealing a vast and luminous fictive terrain without limiting what is possible within it. In the work of Hoke, Kaschock, and Rohrer, this graceful movement between revelation and concealment is most visible in their treatment of familiar narrative structures. We are uncertain whether the "pursuit" is ending or beginning, as the reader almost always finds herself "where it all began." "You will wonder if it was the threshold," Kaschock explains. In each of these beautifully rendered collections, uncertainty becomes a "window," an "entrance," and an "invention."

Hoke's *Genevieves* reads as a ledger of what cannot, will not, be said aloud. Presented as a series of intricately linked hybrid texts, which are each themselves comprised of discrete episodes, Hoke's writing allows uncertainty to accumulate in the space between things. These absences, the "silent" and "unsmiling" gaps between prose narratives, articulate—through their expertly-timed jump cuts and ruptures—a question that is refined over the course of the larger collection. In this subtle and beguiling book, Hoke asks what happens when we refuse to speak, whether this refusal constitutes an end—to discovery, knowledge, and self-actualization—or possibility, a beautiful "doorway" opening "with a flourish."

Reminiscent of early twentieth-century experimental films, particularly their creators' predilection for montage, Hoke reminds us that silence, and the subsequent lack of a clear narrative, make space for the other, inviting "the Crowd" in all of its problematic splendor into the room. He writes, for example, in the first section of this haunted and haunting collection:

> Weaponize your juvenilia.
>
> There are only so many times you can come home before you have to decide why you're there. Before you have to decide when you're getting away. Carolina sat.
>
> There was a soft cough outside her door. Carolina opened it a crack and met her half-brother for the first time.
>
> I've also been hiding, he said. (11)

Hoke offers a seamless matching of style and content, as the preponderance of secrets in this Southern family is enacted within the behavior of the language itself. Here the connections between things, the transitional language we are so accustomed to, is purposefully admitted. For example, each sentence, and the widening expanses between them, asks of the reader a leap in logic, point of view, and syntax. This movement between perspectives is perhaps most visible when the speaker's half-brother walks through the door ("I've also been hiding…"). Like a door opening inside what we thought was a single room, the narrative generates possibility through these abrupt shifts in rhetorical modes, and the line of reasoning that each one represents. As Hoke's prose ambulates between ways of seeing, and the elisions they give rise to, we are prompted—inevitably, irrefutably—to locate ourselves in this gorgeous imagined topography. Hoke himself explains, "As I slip below the waves I'll see light."

Kaschock's *Confessional Sci-Fi: A Primer* continues this engagement with concealment and its seemingly infinite possibilities for readerly participation. Here, too, the transitional language we have come to expect is skillfully hidden from view. We are offered a montage "brimming with chocolates," "cigarettes," and "dipped carnations," all stripped of their narrative artifice, that unnecessary ornamentation (17–19). Similar in structure to *Genevieves*, Kaschock's discrete prose texts represent a dialogue between facets of the same voice, or parts of the same consciousness, rather than a conventionally unified narrative. Her elliptical and gorgeously fractured texts—and the echoing space between them—also becomes metaphor, instructing us as to how the work should be read, engaged with, imagined with.

For Kaschock, all of thought is a conversation, evoking what Mikhail Bakhtin described as "the dialogic imagination." Just as she responds to and interrogates her own observations, deconstructing the various ways of seeing that she inhabits, Kaschock prompts her reader to do the same. Consider the transition between sections in "After Museum,"

> To the museum's visitors (a collective to which you now belong) the two-way guide is a winged primate, atrophying.

The first room is one woman. A strung-out. She is laid on a loom, and her
eyes have accepted this.

Kaschock's presentation of the "woman" reads as a response to the images
of community that are presented in the first stanza—that "collective to
which you now belong." As the poem unfolds, she refines these recurring
questions of choice and agency, considering our roles as readers and consum-
ers of mass culture. More specifically, the text posits the human mind as a
museum, exhibiting the various ephemera, cultural symbols, and pieces of
language that have accumulated within it—mementos that we have not
necessarily chosen ourselves. As "the museum's visitors" wander Kaschock's
display of elusive, elliptical hybrid creations, they become themselves cura-
tors, and Kaschock is implicated in her own incisive, thought-provoking
cultural critique. Yet the moment we think we have discerned intent, "it all
flies outside and into the porchlight like moths, of course and forever...."

❧

Wonderfully ambitious and fully realized, Rohrer's *The Others* engages
similar questions of readerly participation and, more specifically, the cultivation of a shared consciousness through art. In the book's sprawling fictive
terrain, the constant presence of the other within the self—that eternal
alterity—is a shadow story that haunts the narrative proper. As the work
unfolds, it is this secret, hidden most of all from the speaker of the poem,
that is gradually revealed, understood, and dramatized beautifully in the
style of the writing itself.

Early in the poem, Rohrer's speaker makes frequent reference to "the
others," speculating about their inner lives. "At least I always assumed the
others hated their jobs too," he writes (1). Here, and elsewhere in the opening
pages, we encounter a clear divide between subject and object that is skillfully interrogated, and incisively deconstructed. The polyphonic, collectively
voiced style of the poem complicates this line of thinking, positing all of
thought, and our life in language, as a shared endeavor. The project often

takes the form of a linguistic collage, a carefully orchestrated assemblage of attributed language. For example, he writes,

> 'It wasn't real, I think,
> but I saw it for sure.
> The image was broadcast
> To my brain to see it.
> So I saw it, I guess.
>
> 'Well, that's not really much
> of a ghost story, Ron.
> I've actually got one.
> Can I tell it to you?' (108)

In much the same way that the story takes up haunting as one of its primary considerations, we are made to see voice as persistently inhabited by language and rhetoric that is not one's own. This idea manifests perhaps most visibly in Rohrer's use of dialogue. This passage, like many others in the collection, transitions swiftly between quoted sections, the narrative arising from what is really a chorus of voices, a vocal and dissonant collective. With that in mind, his technique not only becomes commentary on the narrative, but rather, it becomes the narrative. It is this provocative tension—between what is explicitly stated and all that is implied by the behavior of the language itself—that drives the collection. What's more, this disconnect, this gorgeous complexity becomes an aperture, a doorway through which the reader may enter the work's vast and radiant fictive topography.

Much like Hoke and Kaschock, Rohrer purposefully refuses exposition, bringing to mind Objectivist poets like Oppen, Niedecker, and Zukofsky. Yet *The Others* situates this rich artistic tradition in a dialogue with more recent conceptual writing and the lyric, ultimately refining their initial question, that lingering doubt as to whether the aesthetic imagination can exist in isolation. Rohrer shows us that the voice arises within the context of a community, and that we are indebted to it, whether or not we fully realize it. As Rohrer himself reminds us, "the gate is already down / and the trap has been sprung" (23).

On Collective Acts of Forgetting
Elizabeth Lyons, Lisa Olstein, & Carolina Ebeid

WALTER BENJAMIN ONCE observed in *Philosophy: Destruction and Experience* that "what has been forgotten...is never something purely individual" (75). It is easy to overlook the fact that memory and its elisions are collectively orchestrated, as we constantly borrow, appropriate, and revise material from a shared cultural imagination. Yet, given the presence of a communal consciousness, forgetfulness also becomes something of an impossibility. What is erased from the master narrative inevitably manifests in other ways, making its presence known in the minutiae of language, syntax, and grammar. What is left out of the tableau remains woven into its canvas; it is housed, projected, and performed in the texture of language, which functions as a shared unconscious of sorts.

Three poetry collections of innovative writing by women consider this notion of syntax as collective memory, as archive, as ledger. Elizabeth Lyons' *The Blessing of Dark Water*, Carolina Ebeid's *You Asked Me to Talk About the Interior*, and Lisa Olstein's *Late Empire* each consider, albeit through a different conceptual lens, the question of what trauma and violence is housed in the words we use. "I am in a room, labeled difficult," Lyons writes (iii). In each of these stunningly crafted collections, we are shown the social upheavals and the deeply personal grief woven into the very rules of language, that glittering "machine" turning just beneath the surface of a community.

This enduring interest in our collective imagining, and even more importantly, what lies at its peripheries, is gorgeously visible in these writers' reframing of silence as a vehicle for institutional critique. Here, the orders of power are jostled and rearranged. We are made to see the absence of narrative as injustice, as violation, as homage, as resistance and feminist gesture. As Lyons herself writes, "I recover. We don't speak of it" (iii).

In *The Blessing of Dark Water*, language is sedimented with history. "I feign deafness," Lyons writes in the opening poem (iii). The formality of the word *feign* renders us startlingly aware that the passing of time transfigures the most ordinary speech acts. As the book unfolds, we are made to see that the boundaries between speech and the unspeakable, narrative and what cannot, will not be said, are also temporally situated.

Lyons brilliantly reminds us that many narratives, particularly the stories of women who breach boundaries and challenge our thinking, could not be voiced in the historical moment that they themselves inhabited. There was not yet a vocabulary, a form, or an appropriate architecture to hold such unruly content, a missive that challenged—and still challenges—our most familiar ontological categories. Throughout the narrative, these limiting, constraining categories of being still loom large: "...my mother / showed me off to a friend as we waited for a / movie to start. Held up my left hand in hers— / Married! Married! Getting Married! My saddest daughter fixed!" (43–44). Throughout the sequence, Lyons draws on hybrid forms reminiscent of the works of Jenny Boully, Yedda Morrison, and Jill Magi to forge a new lexicon, one that can encompass a more robust conceptualization of identity.

In the first part of the sequence, entitled "A Beginning," we as readers are uncertain if we are inhabiting past or present, historical truth or its fictive projection. We gradually realize that it is all of these, as Lyons shows us the way that history, its violence, and its upheavals are carried with us, in the words we use. She elaborates,

> I draw a tree in chalk to signify the forest behind my home. I draw a body of the girl who was, before an illness. I draw a body for the Elizabeth who feigns politeness when it's necessary.
>
> I'm ready at the board, eraser in hand (vi).

The sections, for the most part, are clearly marked with dates indicating past or present, but here, that space is left intentionally blank. We are shown an interstitial space as time becomes elliptical, recursive, circular. The language, too, drifts between temporal moments and their specific vocabularies: the contemporary colloquial blurs into high lyricism, which becomes a striking formality, the "quiet but not still" terrain of historical memory (34).

In Carolina Ebeid's *You Ask Me to Talk About the Interior*, the historicity of language that fascinated Lyons becomes a source of strangeness, even wonder. Here, it is the intimacy of address, and the unfamiliarity of each weighted word, that gives the book an aura of the uncanny. Subtly and skillfully, Ebeid shows us that the distance between past and present, between self and other, and between the text and its reader, is luminous, bright, and infinite. What's more, this vast expanse can be glimpsed in the space between each word, in the distance that the lyric must traverse in order to reach its singular, inevitable "you."

For instance, Ebeid writes,

> A girl reading a letter at an open window,
> the air enters scented with pavement
>
> that hasn't yet set. She'll curve the paper
> into the shape of a nautilus & listen
> into the sea captivity, its stammerings. (6)

Here, we are shown self as world, as "nautilus" and "sea captivity," a vast terrain, where it is impossible to impart full knowledge of its geography to another, even if it were our wish to do so. What's more, Ebeid reminds us that history in all of its complexity is housed within that seemingly small "curve" of "paper" that is the individual consciousness. The mind, for Ebeid, is a ledger, one that has been written over with the "letters" and "open windows" of Romanticism and the "stammerings" of urban industrial modernity. Because of the vastness held within each one of us, Ebeid suggests, subtly and skillfully, the distance between self and other grows that much greater. What's more, intimacy becomes something of an impossibility, as the innermost rooms of the psyche are filled by the objects and ephemera of history, our shared narratives and their myriad philosophical problems, their many injustices.

Ebeid's great gift is her ability to portray this tension between the individual self and a shared historical imagination with beauty, lyricism, and compassion. She reminds us that despite our ultimate isolation, our deep solitude within the walls of the body, the road is lined with "tulips showing their brilliant throats" (6).

Late Empire continues this interrogation of language as vestige, as master narrative in ruins, as archive and as collective unconscious. Much like Ebeid and Lyons, Olstein calls attention to the fragmentation—of meaning, of story, and of voice—housed within syntactic constructions that offer an illusion of wholeness, that deceptive aura of unity and cohesion. In many ways, the tension that Olstein creates between a unified form and this unruly content speaks to the role of grammar, and its implicit logic, in structuring the narratives that circulate within our culture, that echo within each one of us, the stories that ultimately make us ourselves.

For Olstein, grammar implies a very particular type of causation, one that assumes a linear understanding of history, a logic of cause and effect. What is brilliant and provocative about Olstein's work is that she fully acknowledges the impossibility of forgetting a conceptual framework that has been fully internalized, and the futility of fashioning something wholly new. Rather, she realizes that the rules of language must be questioned, interrogated, and revised from within. She elaborates in "Air Rights,"

> One way to think of it is
> I require absence and you are
> lifelong a room just left. Except
> you bloom not empty half-light
> but a stand of trees at the edge
> of the meadow where my life
> leaks out.... (18)

Here, Olstein offers sentences that fit together from a grammatical standpoint, functioning as pristine subject-verb-object constructions. Yet within that flawless grammar, we discover a provocative fragmentation of meaning. For example, as we move into the third line, the semantic meaning of words is no longer privileged, but rather, their musicality, their sonic qualities, becomes the driving logic behind each clause, each gorgeously ruptured sentence. With that in mind, Olstein offers a vision of history in which language becomes an internalization of empire, the mind itself being colonized by a logic and a worldview that is not our own. What is fascinating about *Late Empire* is that Olstein does not merely offer critique, but begins the difficult work of creating an alternative space, an understanding of language that allows for the hypothetical, the disruptive, the utopian.

Like Lyons and Ebeid, Olstein offers us language that is startlingly conscious of its own movement through history. In doing so, each of these writers forges her own ethics and her own lexicon. These are books that remind us what is possible in the most familiar grammars, showing us the strangeness and wonder that resides just beneath a docile surface, the syntax we thought we knew.

Textual Difficulty as a Feminist Gesture

Laurie Sheck, Sarah Vap, & Julia Story

IN HIS WRITINGS on the experience of cultural otherness, Georges Bataille once observed that the marginalized body exists at the periphery of a community, as it cannot be safely contained within or held outside it. Within the context of Bataille's work, otherness is defined as a separation, a visible rupture between the subject and the society that they inhabit.[5] In such a way, marginalized groups function as a veiled threat to the establishment, a population that cannot be housed within its discourse, and thus kept and controlled. More frequently, though, difference is invoked by those in power as a justification for oppression, a reason for exclusion and the ongoing marginalization of voices and perspectives.

For many feminist practitioners, the experience of otherness is an inexorable condition of inhabiting language. Each sentence, with its clean subject-verb-object constructions, enacts a particular kind of logic, a causation rooted firmly in a predominantly male, and predominantly Western, philosophical tradition. In her landmark essay, "The Laugh of the Medusa," Hélène Cixous describes this type of syntax as "marked writing," a toxic masculinity that is exorcised onto language, and borne into the realms of art, of fiction, and the imagination. Perhaps for this reason, found forms, invented forms, hybrid texts, and unclassifiable works are seeing a renaissance in the hands of women and nonbinary writers. More than ever, feminist practitioners are attempting to write outside of, beyond, and against this "marked writing," its linear and logical structure, and the undoubtedly narrow philosophical tradition that it takes for granted.

In recent years, a vibrant artistic landscape, populated with multifarious hybrid writing by women and nonbinary authors, has taken a turn for the dense, the difficult, the forbidding, and the inaccessible. In an article in *Map Magazine*, a staff writer observes, "Experimental prose is difficult—challenging in the way that foreign language learning is challenging." This is because the rules of language, its implicit logic and causal structures, are often reconfigured. As in the work of Lisa Olstein, Sarah Ann Winn, Julia Story, Laurie Sheck, and many other contemporary experimental writers, the sentences fit together, but the words don't cohere in the way that we think they should. We are offered clean syntactic constructions that resist the implicit logic of grammar. Disorder begins to inhabit the orderly linguistic structures we once thought we knew.

Though many critics have written on women's poetry and social justice, few have considered this kind of textual difficulty as a feminist gesture. More often than not, this kind of denseness is seen as a failure—to be understood, to master the forms of discourse, to communicate effectively. Of course, you are likely thinking several things: There is no point in creating a text that is difficult, if not impossible, to understand. If women and nonbinary writers inhabit a marginal space in the literary community, as evidenced by year after year of the VIDA Count, this aesthetic arguably contributes to the continued relegation of feminist texts to the outermost boundaries of the literary world.

The difficult text constitutes a provocative reversal of power, a show of agency and resistance. The feminist practitioner is no longer the outsider, othered within a linguistic terrain that is hostile to her, but instead, she chooses who is granted access into the imaginative world that she constructs, one dense, impenetrable, labyrinthine paragraph at a time.

Before posing questions about artistic failure, it is necessary to remember that, as Viet Thanh Nguyen notes in an essay about writing workshops in *The New York Times*, "Literature and power cannot be separated." Every gesture, every move we make in language responds to, reacts against, propagates, or internalizes existing structures of control, influence, and authority. The expectation that a text be accessible to readers who situate themselves within a specific artistic school of thought is yet another manifestation of power and linguistic violence.

In her hybrid text, *End of the Sentimental Journey*, Sarah Vap calls our attention to the striking similarities in how textual bodies and physical bodies are constructed in language. According to Vap, the difficult text is almost always spoken about as though it were a female body, and as though the mostly male readers in the room are entitled to "access" it (19). As the work unfolds, she situates textual difficulty and easiness on a spectrum, challenging us as her audience to find the sweet spot. She returns again and again to the idea of the "payoff," that abiding belief that a text should give in to the reader, but only after the reader has worked for it awhile.

At the periphery of Vap's text is the question of readerly entitlement. Not all texts are intended for every reader, but instead, might be aimed at underground, non-mainstream, or more specialized audiences. To that end, Vap poses the question, "When someone says a poem is difficult, do they mean that the language of the poem, or the mind of the poem, or the sentiment of the poem is not like *his* or *her* language or mind or sentiments?" (11). A reader who demands that a text perform its meaning in a way that they are accustomed to, that is legible in the eyes of the dominant culture, wields their power in a manner that is linguistically hegemonic, all in the name of "good art." In such a way, all the violence that is suffered by female bodies, and the erasure of nonbinary identities, is done again through language, through interpretation, and the orders of power that structure the environments in which we encounter literary works.

With that in mind, a text that denies entry, that frustrates a sense of readerly entitlement, is perhaps the most disruptive of all. The difficult text resists the reading act as a wielding of mastery, and it challenges those who approach interpretation as a show of mastery and dominance. What's more, it enacts and performs a separatist mentality that has surfaced and resurfaced throughout radical political movements.

Through syntax, through the dexterous movement between registers and discourses, and through form, many feminist practitioners are saying, quite simply: This text is not, was never, intended for *you*.

᙭

This particular variety of textual difficulty, an inaccessibility that is both artistically competent and politically charged, takes many forms, ranging from narrative obfuscation to formal subversion, and challenges the logic and reasoning implicit in the sentence. In the work of Julia Story, the page becomes a visual field, as the writer highlights the containment of her own voice within a legible form, within the sentence, and within language. Her collection, *Post Moxie*, takes the form of neatly shaped prose boxes, which contain within them labyrinths of intricately, and impressively, crafted language. Yet inside of each prose box, each cleanly shaped linguistic container, we encounter a provocative fragmentation of meaning as most readers have heretofore envisioned it.

"I'm in my membrane-colored sweater and we watch the swirl of generic birds," Story writes. "Tears enter your voice when you tell me how long it's been since you fed them" (37). Grammar is made to house a disintegration of the most familiar ontological categories, ranging from sound to color to the animal world. "Birds" appear as something "generic," mass-produced; the "voice" houses "tear" after "tear," becoming something weighty and tangible, and so on. As the ontological categories begin to disintegrate, the relationship between signifier and signified becomes less clear, as we are no longer sure what these familiar words correspond to in a world outside of language and Moxie's daring artistic imagination. In such a way, possibility accumulates within the text, each elision, each rupture in the rules of syntax creating a proliferation of richly envisioned meaning.

Story shows us, subtly and skillfully, how grammar, its rules and its logic, limits what is possible within the imagination. Yet this critique is housed within the familiar confines of the sentence. For Story, the work of the poet is to expand what is possible within the boundaries of language, to carve a space for an alternative definition of reason, one that is nonlinear, and multifarious in its possibilities. As Vap notes in *End of the Sentimental Journey*, those whose mind, whose sentiment, and whose language does operate in such a way will find the writing "difficult." While I do not mean to negate or deny any reader's primary experience of an experimental text, I am heartened by writers who remind us that there is more than one way to inhabit language, and in doing so, expand our sense of what is possible within it.

⚜

Like Story's collection, Laurie Sheck's *A Monster's Notes* explores and upholds obfuscation as a feminist gesture. What is withheld from the reader, both within the narrative and when considering the logic that governs the book, becomes a source of power and agency for the feminist practitioner.

Taking the life and work of Mary Shelley as its subject, *A Monster's Notes* and its obfuscation of meaning speaks to the situation of women inhabiting that particular historical moment. In quite a literal way, the tasks of speaking and being heard were difficult. "If I could hear my voice move outside my mind," her protagonist laments, "but even now this voiceless and all these years later" (414). Sheck's prose literally performs and enacts the difficulty of speaking as a female-identifying subject, and involves the reader within this narrative, as we strain to hear, despite our rapt attention, transfixed by the work's lush and intricately rendered descriptive passages.

The work's monstrous subject matter offers a wry commentary on the ways we as a culture have conceptualized, and continue to limit what is possible for, the marginalized voice. "She had given her creature/monster/being books to wander in and learn from," Sheck tells us. Just as the monster exists in the space between ontological categories, the voice of the novel sprawls outside of received, legible, and modest forms of discourse, become something unrecognizable. The text performs monstrousness through the vastness of the terrain that it claims, its repertoire of innumerable forms and textures of language. Of course, this vastness might be construed as difficulty, the physical object that is the book becoming a veritable saint's burden to carry from one place to the next. For Sheck, it is this monstrous impulse that can dismantle all that is problematic with language, and its radical confusion, making way for something new.

As Sheck herself asks, "Who isn't monsterized" (99).

⚜

And so the feminist text becomes monstrous, unwieldy, no longer dainty or well behaved. Its meaning sprawls outside of, and beyond, the familiar structures of grammar. Such a text is unlike anything we have seen before, its alterity writ large in the very texture of its language. If we begin to conceptualize difficulty as difference, as a performance of and reaction against being pushed up to the margins, what does that open up within our reading of innovative texts by women and nonbinary authors? After all, the politics of textual difficulty are inextricable from their aesthetics.

Even more importantly, a text that challenges us in this way threatens revolution starting at the very foundations of society: the rules of language itself.

Textual Difficulty
A Performance of Otherness & Difference

IN HER HYBRID text, *End of the Sentimental Journey*, Sarah Vap asserts that "we spend our lives both translating into and refusing, to some degree or another, (the nonexistent) Standard American English" (11). Here Vap portrays language as being necessary to the cultivation of community, as its common ground makes possible shared experience, collective memory, and a larger cultural imagination. At the same time, Vap reminds us that grammar necessitates some degree of conformity, as its structures privilege the collective over the individual, silencing the female subject's lingering impulse to question, and reinforcing her lack of agency through the very structure of communication itself.

Through their refusal to conform to normative ideas about how language should behave, two hybrid texts by women offer a point of entry to a necessary discussion of textual difficulty as an aesthetic gesture. Karla Kelsey's *A Conjoined Book* and Gillian Conoley's *The Plot Genie* perform, through their gratifying denseness and purposeful withholding of narrative context, a visible celebration of linguistic otherness and difference. Though somewhat different in their stylistic approach, Conoley and Kelsey both frame textual difficulty as a veritable reversal of power. Though the poet's alterity is palpable in the texture of the language itself, it is she who decides who is and who is not allowed into the imaginative terrain she has created. The text's difficulty becomes a gatekeeping mechanism, rendering the poet's intellectual labor inaccessible to a dominant culture that has only stifled her voice.

The impulse to wield power in such a way calls into question a sense of readerly entitlement, the abiding belief that a text will perform its meaning in a straightforward way, remaining all the while useful to a culture that operates on exclusion, systemic iniquities, and abuses of power. By refusing to render their writing serviceable to the dominant culture, and all but denying access, Kelsey and Conoley begin work toward a separate rhetorical space, in which the female subject retains greater agency with respect to who her language serves, and who may engage with the work of her heart and her mind. As Kelsey herself writes, "I ply the narrative out at acute angles, a hush fallen over the line of children following a tractor engraving red clay" (18).

Karla Kelsey's *A Conjoined Book* takes readerly expectations as one of its primary considerations, confronting them head-on through its innovative approach to poetic technique. For Kelsey, the beauty of the "conjoined book" is the implicit questioning of a preconceived notion that language should be uniform in its texture, when in actuality, it is in the friction, the elisions, and the space between rhetorical modes where possibility truly lies. Part of the book's potential difficulty is its quick movement from one mode of representation to the next, becoming almost cinematic in its use of montage and jump cuts. Yet these small apertures become a liminal space, in which the rules of language no longer hold.

"Dresses scattered along the interstate," Kelsey writes, "Silk and calico" (22). Throughout the book, the threat of violence exists at the periphery, evoking the cruelty implicit in language, its privileging of a collective that is at its core unjust. As the sequence unfolds, Kelsey reveals grammar as a form of violence done to voice and narrative, a visible rupture that is enacted in, and reconstituted by, the work's swift movement between lexicons. Kelsey writes in one of the book's episodic "Afterimage" poems,

> The window bathed in blue & the window bathed in
> tourmaline. How to approach a series of photographs
> torn from event, a collection of wounded nexuses.
> Evidence of antecedents, discontinuities between them
> laboring over a continuous dawn. (21)

This passage is revealing in its presentation of ontological violence, that meaning "torn from its event," that "wounded nexus." For Kelsey, there is a malice inherent in dictating the direction that reasoning takes, that luminous arc of narrative unfolding in a traditionally legible way. By embracing the "discontinuities" and "laboring" in the aperture "over a continuous dawn," she reminds us instead of the generative violence implicit in the experiment. As Kelsey herself observes, "A rift in the landscape of memory, even when she tapes the images together" (22).

Conoley's *The Plot Genie*, like Kelsey's *A Conjoined Book*, distinguishes carefully between the violence implicit in linguistic convention and the generative violence of the experiment. For Conoley, too, tradition must be torn apart in order to be redeemed. Part of the text's difficulty arises from the fragmentary nature of the text, its ephemeral movement between forms and rhetorical modes. As the book unfolds, we are presented with prose poems, visual texts, lineated verse, and hybrids of all kinds, with none of the expected narrative scaffolding. Yet this elision is the work's most provocative gesture, as Conoley, like Kelsey, calls attention to the unique opportunities inherent in liminal textual spaces.

As tradition is dismantled, Conoley proffers the fragment as a zone of possibility, existing in the space between literary convention and innovation. Without the unwieldy apparatus of its artistic lineage, the fragment can be borne into new territory, becoming something else through its recontextualization. Conoley writes, for example, in "Dear R.,"

> Comedy Boy came by horseback with your letter,
>
> his head appeared then disappeared in woods receding
>
> as he rode
>
> between trees, in chambers dim with histories,
>
> times a shaft of sun would fall on his pale hair […]

Here Conoley summons the ghost of Romantic poets like Keats and Shelley, portraying the sublime as being at once beautiful, painful, and unattainable. Yet this familiar vision of the Romantic dark sublime is borne into a feminist tradition of hybrid writing, that refusal to inhabit a tradition that is hostile to one's voice. For Conoley, the text's difficulty is crucial for this process of transformation, as the denseness—of language, of forms, of allusions and referents—in effect defamiliarizes that which we once thought we knew. As Conoley herself writes, "Keats could feel all this in his lungs."

If textual difficulty is a conscious choice, our motivations are both adversarial and optimistic. To write toward a more just way of inhabiting language, in many ways, entails some degree of difficulty for a potential audience. We, as readers, are not used to language that fails to adhere to the familiar (and arguably patriarchal) rules of meaning-making. For Kelsey and Conoley, the difficult text becomes a show of agency and resistance, a reaction against a conformist approach to inhabiting language. As Conoley herself asserts, "That's precisely how antagonists wreck one's mind."

The Poetics of Disbelief

IN 1817, SAMUEL Taylor Coleridge famously coined the term "suspension of disbelief," meaning a willingness to silence one's critical faculties and believe in something purely conjectural for the sake of art (174). Since the publication of Coleridge's *Biographia Literaria*, his provocative ideas about cognitive estrangement—and the claim that we can so easily abandon the rules that govern our minds and hearts—have become indispensable for our understanding of how we experience works of literature. For Coleridge, some degree of trust in the storyteller, and a willingness on the part of the reader to take risks, is essential for a work of literary art to fully realize its aesthetic potential, to convey its meaning, and to assert its effects on the spectator.

In two hybrid texts, Coleridge's seminal writings on the "suspension of disbelief" are brought to bear on provocative and necessary sociopolitical questions. Paige Ackerson-Kiely's *dolefully, a rampart stands* and Sara Veglahn's *The Ladies* interrogate the structures of power that determine which narratives, and which storytellers, have the privilege of an unwavering trust, that startling absence of skepticism. In the work of these visionary writers, disbelief is revealed as a show of power and, more often than not, an all-too-familiar unwillingness to empower others.

Both Ackerson-Kiely and Veglahn share an investment in shining light on the politics implicit in disbelief and examining its entrenched place in our culture as a tool of disempowerment. This impulse comes through most visibly in the relationship that these writers create between the text and its audience. As their work unfolds, they confront a kind of readerly disbelief, that tacit assumption that female practitioners will be rewarded for certain types of narratives, those stories of love, distress, and triumph that are familiar and culturally legible, while other narratives—and modes of narration—are supposedly suspect. As Ackerson-Kiely herself writes, "I wrote a victim impact statement the way I'd want to hear it" (55).

Ackerson-Kiely's *dolefully, a rampart stands* sketches a landscape in which sexism and economic oppression are indelibly linked. Though her gorgeously rendered lines are filled with female speakers and women characters, the narratives themselves are marked by a striking contentiousness, as Ackerson-Kiely evokes the ways culture divides individuals from historically marginalized groups against themselves, if only to prevent them from rising up.

Ackerson-Kiely reveals the ways that power, censorship, and disbelief are internalized, as they live with us in our most solitary moments, and they circumscribe what is possible within our dreaming. In doing so, she challenges many of the myths of a shared feminist consciousness. For instance, she writes in "Book About a Candle Burning in a Shed,"

> I don't mention the dreams: Roadkill comes back to life, the answers I don't have but am asked for by an angry mob. What we do with details is not unlike touching a thing that doesn't want to be touched, a thing that would wheel around and bite the hand if only it could. The part of hunger we deserve. (50)

The speaker, whose community has borne witness to so much violence, ultimately resists the invitation to narrate it in her own voice, preferring instead the "crackle and splinter" of a distant radio (54). The disbelief that inhabits this fictive town has been gradually internalized, becoming a deep silence, not unlike the "river that moves a body toward its banks" (54).

In Ackerson-Kiely's presentation, this silence and self-censorship arises from an abiding suspicion surrounding women's voices, and stories that fail to adhere to familiar ideas how a life unfolds. In this fictive terrain, master narratives like these are as subtle as they are pervasive. "I know what you're thinking right now," Ackerson-Kiely writes in "Laconia," "It's true she took her first job after high school. What can you do" (13). Here, and throughout the book, she reacts against the assumptions that the reader likely brings to the poem, their belief that they can situate images, archetypes, and symbols within a framework culled from a shared cultural memory. Though acknowledging the familiar features of the story, Ackerson-Kiely does not want us to limit what is possible within it. "You were given everything," she tells the reader in "Meadow Redaction" (26). Now they will learn to be a good steward of the gift.

Veglahn's *The Ladies* continues this interrogation of disbelief and its implicit power dynamics. She shows us, subtly and skillfully, that the boundaries between self and other, and the perceived ownership of language and narrative, are often a precondition for readerly belief. Presented as a polyphonic text, in which a mysterious "we" plans, documents, and sings a revolution into being, the story takes as one of its central questions the relationship between the individual and the collective.

Within Veglahn's richly imagined text, the women's voices that comprise the chorus, the luminous "us" that populates these discrete prose episodes, never break away from the group. As the story unfolds, we begin to wonder whether they are encountering a multitude, or a self that contains within it multitudes. Like Ackerson-Kiely, Veglahn gestures at the ways shared culture, and its implicit power dynamics, give rise to a consciousness that is, at its core, divided.

Veglahn writes,

> In the chapels. In the cathedrals. In the small country churches. In the basements of churches. In their rooms in the dark. In their kitchens. In their doorways and hallways. Inside our heads. In our minds, they spoke. They spoke through us. We do not know how to explain this. It was not like voices. It was not like thought. (91)

Here Veglahn confronts and reacts against the readerly assumption of a unified self, a self that can claim ownership over their place in language. She resists this kind of textual ownership as a precondition for belief, that willing suspension of skepticism. "Inside our chests something was burning," Veglahn tells us, "We couldn't identify what it was. We couldn't get it out"

(41). Like Ackerson-Kiely, Veglahn makes the reader suddenly and startlingly aware of the limitations they place on language before it has a chance to unfold before them. For both Ackerson-Kiely and Veglahn, it is the master narrative, that "small container," that limits the possibilities for belief, trust, and the creation of community (41).

If univocal utterance is a precondition for readerly belief, then what of the storyteller that contains within her the world? How do we create fictions when our voices have been halved by a flawed culture, its abuses of power, and their inevitable internalization? For Veglahn and Ackerson-Kiely, seeing, and fully acknowledging, these rifts and fissures is a first step toward change. These writers, through their experimentation with poetic voice and readerly participation, remind us that a leap of faith can open up rooms within what we once thought was a single room—a chapel of light that has been there all along.

An Afterword

On Being the Spectacle
The Sexualization of Women's Labor in the Small Press

1.

IT IS NO secret that women's work in the small press is often read by our male colleagues as a performance of desire, a kind of masquerade that appropriates and irreverently reconstitutes the conventions of academic spaces. Through the refraction of the cis male gaze, an invitation to "contribute"—or worse, to "collaborate"—becomes, for many men, an exploration of boundaries, power, and a deeply unsettling culture of literary celebrity.

To illustrate this problem, I would like to share an anecdote that is all too commonplace in the literary community. I showed up to a colleague's reading in a nice dress, and crossed paths with a poet, with whom I had collaborated professionally. He demanded to know what I was doing there, near that building, at *exactly* the same time that he was standing there. Though I explained that my colleague was giving a reading, he persisted in his belief that I was there, in a nice dress, *for him*.

In reality, we as women in the small press, are working. Our language, our curatorial projects, and our insights are our livelihood. Still, it has become commonplace for cis men in the literary community to read our economic sustenance and survival—as we pass through the halls of the colleges where we adjunct, as we respond to submissions, and as we organize features and roundtables—as a grand romantic gesture, as a signification of sexual accessibility, a poorly crafted pickup line written in lemon juice.

More often than not, sex is perceived as being at the very center of our interactions, when in reality, survival is the endgame, the object of every wish and fantasy. Which is to say, this work I am doing, the labor that wrecks the nerves in my seemingly delicate hands, is not, was never, intended for you.

2.

As it happens, the problem always begins in language. Many critics have articulated, and continue to stand by, a disturbing correlation that has been drawn between the physical body and textual body, in which the poem, essay, or story is seen as an extension or appendage of its author. Within this problematic conceptual framework, when a woman solicits the work, she solicits the physical body of that writer, in all of its slouching, argyle, and undoubtedly awkward postures.

A literature survey of work published in the field of hermeneutics will return innumerable books and articles with titles like "Text as Body, Body as Text," "The Body as Text: A Psychological and Cultural Reading," "The Body as Cultural Text," and so on. When scholars speak about literature, this mindset is as deeply entrenched as it is disturbing. Variations on this same perspective range from Donald Hall referring to poetic form as "The Sensual Body" (32) to Michael McClure describing poetics as a kind of "meat science." Cary Nelson adeptly summarizes this discourse in a critical study, noting that "[t]he idea of the poem *as* body or as direct expression of psychic and physiological ratios characterizes one dominant mode of poetry...forged around the authenticity of expression guaranteed by the signifying body" (590).

What has this discourse meant for women? I believe that this conceptual framework has had unwanted, and deeply felt, repercussions for not only women's poetry, but for the communities in which they strive to develop their work, learn, and mentor others.

More often than not, when we as women express intellectual interest, this curiosity is read through the lens of physical desire, and in this way we are de-intellectualized by our male peers within a small press community that claims to have democratized self-expression for all. When a woman says, *I love your book*, it is all too often translated by male writers as that familiar beacon of hope and wishful thinking: *I love you*.

To position any text as a projection of the physical body is reductive, as it limits expression to what is material and tactile, altogether negating what Paul Ricœur called the "symbolic" dimensions of language.[6] Within Freudian theory, this is where meaning "crystalizes," gaining denseness and complexity; for Ezra Pound, this rhetorical space gives rise to the "emotional and intellectual complex" that the reader then unravels (202). The symbolic realm is where meaning and possibility multiply, and where poetry actually *happens*. The danger of framing language as mere physical utterance, rather than a more complex process of signification, is that one forecloses many of the intellectual planes to which language can deliver us.

What's more, this desire to give the material body primacy over language is as misguided as it is dangerous. It invites a kind of biological essentialism into our academic and professional spaces, a mindset that does not challenge us to examine the ways we speak about gender, sexuality, and the visceral, tangible power dynamics within these settings. As Raewyn Connell notes in *Feminism's Challenge to Biological Essentialism*,

> Curiously, whatever biological mechanism was appealed to, the argument always ended up in the same place: Conventional sex roles, gender divisions of labour, and inequalities of power, were biologically determined and therefore could not be challenged. Feminist activism was coming up against nature and so, ultimately, it was futile.

The body itself exists as a discursive construction, arguably even more so than it does as a tangible thing. After all, it is language that gives meaning, coherence, and order to our most visceral perceptions. In his book on corporeality and social theory, Chris Shilling, in *The Body and Social Theory*, goes so far as to describe the body as an "absent presence," noting the importance of language in constituting our relationship to our physical being (17). Lesley Jeffries even claims in *Textual Construction of the Female Body* that the "role of the body is being taken by language" (xi).

The tendency to read women's writing as merely a performance of physical desire becomes, then, a kind of reduction of language itself, an essentialism that diminishes the intellect, reducing the elegant metaphor to innuendo, an aesthetic gesture to suggestion, and metonymy to Nabokovian disembodiment.

3.
The Sexualization of Women's Labor in the Small Press
A Partial Archive

"Damn. When you said you loved my work, I thought you meant something better."

"Your poems are like fruits, Kristina. They're just begging to be squeezed."

"I *knew* you wanted more than just a copy of my book."

"I like the way you break your lines."

"Yours fondly."

" 'sup."

4.

In the context of the #MeToo movement, it is crucial to note the relationship between textual violence and bodily violence. As Luce Irigaray notes in *This Sex Which Is Not One*, the breach of boundaries, and the subsequent violation, almost always begins in language. Indeed, signification often functions as a hypothetical testing ground, a separate space in which tangible boundaries and palpable relationships are forged, manipulated, or torn apart.

This is not to position language as the body, per se, but to underscore the ways language shapes our demeanor in the physical spaces we pass through in both professional and personal settings. If language, and the work we do with language, is framed as sexually charged, then this conceptual framework amplifies the potential, however muted it may be, for violation.

In his critical study, *Re-Engendering Translation*, Christopher Larkosh notes the tendency to "repeat physical violence through textual violence," and to perpetuate power imbalances though one's discursive construction of the other. I would caution anyone against thinking that physical violence is, in the end, subdued to textual violence in Larkosh's analysis. Rather, there is an active and ongoing reciprocity between language and the visceral power dynamics between people.

Case in point: I spent three years of my young adult life corresponding with an older man, more established in his career than myself. Though he later became physically violent toward me, he first defaced my book and mailed it to me. Language was the first fire, the last light.

There is a deeply entrenched tendency among many cis men to view language through the lens of sexuality, as kind of a prerequisite for establishing power, influence, and gauging where exactly a boundary lies. In recent years, even poetry has been co-opted as a kind of metonymy, standing in for what has not yet, and might never, be said between two people.

Which is to say, the free play of meaning that makes poetry beautiful has been stilled, arrested, all but frozen in place.

Textual Violence & the Workshop
Responding to Difficult Poetry by Women

AN EMPTY CUP, a crumpled paper, my mind already gone from the room. The conversation treading the same paragraph over and over as though it were a body of water. Needless to say, I could not speak.

The only good writer in a workshop is a dead writer. You are a dead writer starting NOW.

As a student, I was obedient. I rarely questioned anyone who spoke with the least bit of authority. Yet the whole time, I remember an unease blossoming beneath my skin. Its petals unfurling one by one as the pages of my manuscript were turned by my classmates.

I cannot seem to enter the text. The text isn't granting me access.
Why can't I enter the text.

At the time of the critique, I had been keenly interested in exploring textual difficulty as a feminist gesture. By then twenty-eight years old, I spent several years bouncing back and forth between various low-residency MFA programs, artist colonies, and noncredit workshops, searching for a sense of artistic community. No matter what landscape, building, or campus, I remained deeply disturbed by one thing: the difficult text was almost always spoken about as though it were a female body, and as though the primarily male readers in the room were entitled to "access" it.

This mindset—the belief that every artistic work should yield to the hand of a reader who attends closely enough to syntax, his pocket Lacan dictionary at arm's reach—was, in my estimation, deeply symptomatic. In recent years, the reading act has ceased to be an exercise in humility but has instead been transfigured into a visible wielding of mastery, a desire to dominate and colonize.

As Teresa D. Lauretis observes in her study of gender and reading practices, "French feminism goes as far as to consider the act of interpretation a patriarchal enterprise, the goal of which is to achieve power or mastery over a given text. In this theoretical schema, the text is identified with femininity, and interpretation becomes a way of arresting the free play of meaning analogous to the way patriarchy contains women and women's sexuality" (126).

In so many of these classroom discussions, the text is made to stand in for the female body, and all the violence that is suffered by female bodies, here, is done again through language, through interpretation, and through the orders of power that undergird the settings in which this feedback is given.

⚜

Of course, many of the poems I submitted for the requisite critiques intentionally violated readerly expectations. I reacted against the abiding belief that as a younger female writer, I was expected to give a certain amount of emotion, not more, not less.

In her book *End of the Sentimental Journey*, Sarah Vap describes the fraught relationship between the reading act and what she calls a payoff. According to Vap, readers need a text to be just easy enough. That is, readers generally like to feel as though the text has given into them, but also they like to feel that they've worked for it.

She situates textual difficulty and easiness on a spectrum, asking the reader to find the sweet spot.

Certainly, Vap calls our attention to the similarities in how textual bodies and physical bodies are constructed in language. The challenge to us as her audience, then, was to exist beyond or outside of this conversation. To forge a new vocabulary, a new syntax, a lexicon that's more hospitable to innovation by women.

For me, this feminist utopia had already become a republic of one.

x x x x

We tend to forget that the workshop model of creative writing instruction is predicated on disenfranchisement. We watch as others attempt to gain visible mastery over our voices, our aesthetic predilections, our lives in language, and in most pedagogical settings, we are not allowed to interject. For individuals who come from a demographic in society that has been silenced, denied, or disempowered in some way, the workshop model often appears as yet another manifestation of power and violence.

The only good writer in a workshop is a dead writer. You are a dead writer starting NOW…

In an essay, Viet Thanh Nguyen notes in a *New York Times* article that "Literature and power cannot be separated. American literature is read around the world not only because of its inherent value, but because the rest of the world always reads the literature of empires." The workshop model of instruction often functions as an extension of empire, facilitated by those who have vested stakes in the current orders of power.

Yes, of course, graduate students need to learn how to receive constructive feedback gracefully, to listen, and speak only when it is their turn. But the usual workshop pedagogy affects different types of artistic practitioners in dissimilar, often incommensurable, ways. It is perhaps most problematic for a writer working outside of legible and familiar forms, attempting to effect social change through the very foundations of society: language itself.

As an experimental feminist practitioner, I often felt as though I were staring the status quo in the face during my class critiques. After all, nearly 90% of full-time faculty in such settings are white, and well over 70% are white men.

⁂

Workshop Violence: A Partial Archive

"The speaker of the poem is not a likeable girl."

"No. You have to understand. Kristina chose this found language and the fact that she chose it, well, this says something about her."

"Kristina's poems are an insult to her accomplished collaborator's intelligence."

"I don't understand why Kristina writes in broken forms. Maybe this means she was the victim of sexual violence at some point."

"Writing a feminist response to Shakespeare is elitist. And classist. I mean, you have to have gone to a college and read Hamlet to get the poem."

"Who cares."

"Actually…"

"I think the poem is about…"

⚜

In my nearly ten years in graduate school, what disturbed me most about workshops were the moments in which the writing served as merely vehicle, a vast storehouse of language from which men (and sometimes women) could craft pickup lines. Textual and bodily conquest were indelibly linked for many aspiring and mid-career practitioners.

A survey mentioned in *Inside Higher Ed* found that 38% of female respondents in graduate programs have been sexually harassed by men in a position of authority over their academics. The percentage that includes harassment by male peers is much larger.[7]

I haven't heard from you in a couple of months, Kristina. Now tell me whether or not you've had sex with him.

I enrolled in my first workshop because I aspired to better journal publications. Instead, I was surveilled by male poets via the internet, and by their departmental secretaries when they did not have time to surveil me themselves. I witnessed frustrated desire exorcised onto my poems, which in turn became sites of various male poets' catharsis. My poems also served as a mere opportunity for various abuses of power.

You and I should work on a collaboration, Kristina. I think a good first step would be you buying a plane ticket and flying here to have sex with me.

When I mentioned this exchange to my friend, she looked at me and said, "You are clearly just the girl in this batch of girls. Next year there will be a fresh batch."

In late 2012, I was the victim of an attempted assault by my instructor's colleague. He switched my drink at a party, but I wouldn't drink it. In the months that followed, I changed my phone number. Still, he sent me the most terrifying things in the mail.

Needless to say, my writing workshopmates were bludgeoned with angry story after angry story, all of them about young women who looked like me, and who were eventually found dead in the woods.

The class critiques quickly turned into a trial, and my ability as the star witness was called into question:

The language is not compelling when you write about the violence men have done to you.

I don't understand why you would have chosen that dress at all.

No, no, this work is not on the same level as your poems to him about love.

When violence could no longer be enacted on my physical body, the text was again proffered as a substitute, standing in as the object of male aggression.

With that said, I never took my course evaluations. I did not want an institutional record of my trauma because I did not want to see it redacted, written over, or erased.

Readerly Privilege & Textual Violence
Towards an Ethics of Engagement

A HEAP OF dead lilies on the table, that small white envelope, my red dress already torn. The desert and his voice playing over and over in my mind like a film. Now, a quieter room in another landscape. Days later, I would open the envelope. I would tear into it slowly, hear the paper rip from its crackling seams.

By then, I'd moved beyond fright, even when I saw my own handwriting through the postmark. The small sheaf of new work I had sent, shot through with dark blue ink:

You have overestimated yourself....
Keep trying is all that I can say at this point....
A poem should be a symphony of related parts and yours are not nearly there at all....

That's when the air grew even colder. I expected a small pressed flower, perhaps a token or a trinket. I had moved earlier that year to Buffalo to begin work toward a doctorate in literature, while he headed west. Although young, I sensed the imbalance in power, in compassion, in desire. Still, I didn't know what to say. That night, the snow seemed to go on for miles.

In the years to come, I would continue to send him drafts, hoping that one would finally crack the glittering ice that had gathered on my mailbox. Everything returned to me the same way, via FedEx:

Somehow you continue to mask your true feelings, your innermost fears....
I can see how afraid you are of losing control....
Perhaps the perfect relationship for you would be with a man who loved your work....
No, I am not the ideal reader for you....

Yes, I should have walked away. But sometimes the will to believe is even stronger than belief itself.

In the months that followed, I allowed sexually explicit things to be written on my poems. When I failed to respond quickly, I wondered how he obtained my new number. I would look at my smartphone and cry.

Worse yet, this same narrative would become fairly routine for me as I interacted with (somewhat privileged, usually older) male writers.

J. from the Iowa Writers Workshop scrawled expletives across a love poem.

Later, K. would publicly disparage my body of work, only to tell me privately just how compelling it really was.

S. would remove me from the acknowledgments page of his second book, even after I provided extensive comments on five eighty-page drafts. After all, my work wasn't really "known."

S. would also erase my feminist erasure of Vladimir Nabokov's *Lolita*.

Another man would color-code my poems, delineating several "zones of worthwhileness."

I cannot count on two hands the number of times my poems were defaced, erased, or otherwise marked up with a bright red pen. This is not due to a lack of examples, but rather, to the limitations of human anatomy.

Looking back, the questions I would return to most often involved the ethics of reading, particularly when an imbalance of power is at play. It seemed strange to me that the individuals who did violence to my poems were older, white men who attended expensive colleges. At the time, I was a younger female contingent laborer who more than likely qualified for food stamps.

With that in mind, what constitutes violence when responding to a literary text? How does this change when the reader occupies a position of privilege? Is there an ethical way to interact with a text written by a member of a historically marginalized group of people, and what does this look like in practice?

The snow is still towering outside my tiny window. But the ice on my mailbox has just begun to thaw.

❧

Textual violence takes many forms. For me, the most egregious of these violations occurs when the reader makes inferences that extend beyond the work as it appears on the page.

Consider the somewhat polemical review of Kathleen Rooney's book of essays that appeared in *The Rumpus*:

> It is perhaps this obsession with surface and self that does not let Rooney's narratives progress, this constant sinking into the superficial that does not allow her to move deeper. In addition, Rooney seems always be avoiding one food or another, always dancing around eating—a possible disorder that goes begging to be touched upon.[8]

Certainly, there are individuals who assert the importance of negative reviews, and I do believe that writers should be held accountable for the work they publish. Yet what seems most disturbing about this review is the failure to separate the author from the carefully crafted persona that we see in the essays. Any essay certainly involves some degree of artifice, as we choose which facets of ourselves and our experiences to bring to the fore. To attempt to diagnose an author with an eating disorder on the basis of a constructed persona, pure artifice, seems dangerous to me. And completely, undoubtedly irrelevant to the work itself.

When I discovered that this accusation came from a female writer much older than Rooney, I was appalled. Writers should be scrutinized for their work, certainly, but readers should also be held accountable for their privilege, which can take many different forms.

All too often, very personal essays, poems, and fiction become springboards for attacks that are largely personal in nature. This seemed to be the case when my poems were touted as illustrations of my inability to confront my true emotions. This clearly appears to be true of several other reviews, particularly those that deal with Heather Christle's *What Is Amazing*.

For example, Jordan Davis's piece in *The Constant Critic*:

> Only something like a rush to market could have led Christle to invite
> comparison to work universally acknowledged to have changed the art for
> the better.

To comment on the author's perceived marketing strategies when drafting
the poems suggests that we can discern authorial intention through close
readings of individual poems. Furthermore, this passage psychologizes the
author in a way that I find entirely disconcerting.

Yes, most reviewers are well-read, perceptive individuals with impressive
backgrounds in the literary arts. This, however, does not qualify them as
psychiatric professionals.

The same envelope sits on my coffee table. Its edges still ripped from their
seams.

&

Is this textual violence always gendered, and if so, how?

Not always, but more often than not, it is gendered. I present you with
Mark Halliday's review from the winter 2015 issue of *Pleiades*:

> Things have gotten to be so awful, you will need some even scarier meta-
> phors. Will you have enough energy to produce them? You weren't born
> until 1982, so you probably have energy galore. (210)

First of all, this discussion of Traci Brimhall's *Our Lady of the Ruins*
seems overly aggressive in its use of the second person. This stylistic choice
immediately makes the criticism of the work seem personal in nature. Yes,
there is room for creativity in literary criticism, but for an older male poet
to address the author directly in a vaguely menacing tone seems more than
a little problematic to me.

Furthermore, to tout her personal details throughout the review—most
notably her age, which is referenced throughout the piece—gives the impres-
sion that the reviewer is forming judgments about the work based on these
bits of personal data. Otherwise, why mention them?

No, I don't believe that older male writers owe aspiring younger women
positive reviews. But why attempt to silence a demographic in society that
is already more than a little marginalized?

Now, a knock at the door. The FedEx truck is parked outside my apartment.

⚜

What, then, do critics in a position of privilege owe others?

Poetry criticism is an art that should be practiced mindfully and with self-awareness. I continue to be shocked by the extent to which individuals lack any awareness of their privilege.

I believe that reviewers should avoid foreclosing possibilities for individuals to appreciate a given work of art.

On a related note, our biases are often the result of class, race, gender, and our otherwise limited experience of the world around us. Reviewers should not hold up their personal tastes as a normative standard that others should aspire to. Humility is a virtue, after all.

⚜

The reviews that excite me most, and remind me what is possible within literary criticism as an art form, are those that open up new possibilities for individuals who may or may not have encountered the work in question.

With that in mind, I offer you John James' review of *American Barricade*, which appears in the 2014 issue of *Boston Review*:

> Exploring the interplay of economic and psychic obstacles to progress and happiness, the book's calculatedly irregular punctuation and syntax and diverse forms make for a work of perpetual shifting, uncertainty, and dread.

What's interesting about this passage is the critics' concerted effort to situate the work in a larger social and cultural landscape. I admire the ways that this review highlights the potential for stylistic choices in poetry to be read as politically charged, socially relevant, and philosophical. In my opinion, reviews like this one instruct interested readers as to how to approach the work in question, but also they open up new possibilities for individuals who have already encountered the text. I'm deeply invested in reviews that foster a richer experience for readers of poetry, as well as reviews that help literary works reach an appropriate, appreciative audience.

I do believe that there are occasions when critics can, and should, point to a work's failures. More specifically, if a book would likely be unsatisfactory for a particular type of reader, this seems like a legitimate concern to address in a review. Consider Lincoln Greenhaw's discussion of dawn lonsinger's *Whelm*, published in *The Colorado Review*,

> This tendency brings me to my only bone of contention with the book. It can be hard to render inside the reader's skull the sheer number of images implied by many of the lines:
>
> they can hear glaciers
>
> tipping, water rising, maybe
> the ovary-nouns by their own de-
> vice map the water in
>
> our bodies dispersing like shrapnel

But this is a minor issue in light of the book's determination to overwhelm. Underlying such images is the figure of the individual trying to steel itself against the flood of the objective world at one moment, or against a flood of memory the next. The self in the poem is often presented in a contentious relationship to the inanimate world ("the topiary brain—scissored / by shadows"), and the tension between those two elements leads the book to turn inward, to investigate the inanimate elements that make up the subjective self.

What's perhaps most compelling about this review is the way that Greenhaw delineates the readers for whom the book would probably fail, but also names those for whom the work would more than likely succeed. I appreciate Greenhaw's efforts to help the book reach an appreciative audience, while at the same time, serving a gatekeeping function, explaining clearly and detachedly the type of reader who would be better served by another writer's aesthetic.

Reviewers are not arbiters of taste, but rather, they are ushers in a room full of empty chairs. I can only hope they will show us the way.

Notes

1. See Lim, Dennis. "Explaining Movies by Jumping Right Inside Them."
2. See Heynen, Robert and Emily Van der Meulen. *Expanding the Gaze,* p. 106.
3. See Sharif, Solmaz. Note at beginning of *Look.*
4. See Shakespeare, William. *Hamlet.* Act 3, Scene 1.
5. See Brown, Alife. *Losing the Self: Transgression in Lawrence and Bataille.*
6. See Rasmussen, David M. *Mythic-Symbolic Language and Philosophical Anthropology.*
7. See Colleen Flaherty, "Worse Than It Seems.
8. See Garcia, Vanessa. "Vanity Fair." Book review. https://therumpus.net/2010/02/vanity-fair/.

Works Cited

Ackerson-Kiely, Paige. *Dolefully, a Rampart Stands*. Penguin Books, 2019.

Akbar, Kaveh. *Calling a Wolf a Wolf*. Alice James Books, 2017.

Arnold, Mary-Kim. *Litany for the Long Moment*. Essay Press, 2018.

Bakhtin, Mikhail M. "Discourse in the Novel." *The Dialogic Imagination: Four Essays by M. M. Bakhtin*, edited by Michael Holquist. University of Texas Press, 1981, pp. 259–331.

Balakian, Peter. *Ozone Journal*. University of Chicago Press, 2015.

Baran, Jessica. *Common Sense*. Lost Roads Press, 2016.

Barngrover, Anne. *Brazen Creature*. The University of Akron Press, 2018.

Brown, Alfie. "Losing the Self: Transgression in Lawrence and Bataille." *Etudes Laurenciennes*, vol. 43, 2012, pp. 259–280. https://journals.openedition.org/lawrence/105.

Benjamin, Andrew. *Walter Benjamin's Philosophy: Destruction and Experience*. Routledge, 2013.

Benjamin, Walter. "The Metaphysics of Youth." *Walter Benjamin: Selected Writings Volume 1, 1913–1926*, edited by Marcus Bullock and Michael W. Jennings. Belknap Press, 1996, pp. 6–17.

Campanioni, Chris. *The Internet is for Real*. Winston-Salem, C&R Press, 2019.

Carr, Julie. *Real Life: An Installation*. Omnidawn, 2018.

Chang, Victoria. *Barbie Chang*. Copper Canyon Press, 2018.

Champion, Anne. *The Good Girl Is Always a Ghost*. Black Lawrence Press, 2018.

Cixous, Hélène. "The Laugh of the Medusa," trans. Keith Cohen and Paula Cohen, *Signs*, vol. 1, no. 4, 1976, pp. 875–893.

Coleridge, Samuel Taylor. *Biographia Literaria*, 1817. https://www.gutenberg.org/files/6081/6081-h/6081-h.htm.

Connell, Raewyn. "Feminism's Challenge to Biological Essentialism." *Raweyn Connell*, March 2013, http://www.raewynconnell.net/2013/03/feminisms-challenge-to-biological.html.

Conoley, Gillian. *The Plot Genie*. Omnidawn, 2009.

Cummings, Gillian. *The Owl Was a Baker's Daughter*. Center for Literary Publishing, 2018.

Davis, Jordan. "What Is Amazing." *Constant Critic*, 25 Oct. 2012, constantcritic.com/jordan_davis/what-is-amazing/.

de Lauretis T. "Feminist Studies/Critical Studies: Issues, Terms, and Contexts." In de Lauretis T. (eds) *Feminist Studies/Critical Studies. Language, Discourse, Society*. Palgrave Macmillan, 1986.

Derrida, Jacques. *Paper Machine*, Stanford University Press, 2005, p. 28

Dickey, William Michael. *Beyond the Gaze: Post-Foucauldian Surveillance in Fictive Works*. Dissertation, School of Graduate Studies and Research, Indiana University of Pennsylvania, 2011.

Doxsee, Julie. *What Replaces Us When We Go*. Black Ocean, 2018.

Ebeid, Carolina. *You Ask Me to Talk About the Interior*. Noemi Press, 2016.

Ewing, Eve L. *Electric Arches*. Haymarket Books, 2018.

Flaherty, Collen, "Worse Thank It Seems." *Inside Higher Ed*, July 18, 2017.

Freud, Sigmund. *The Interpretation of Dreams*. Plain Label Books, 1953.

Greenhaw, Lincoln. "Whelm." *Center for Literary Publishing*, Colorado State University, 2013, coloradoreview.colostate.edu/reviews/whelm/.

Greenstreet, Kate. *The End of Something*. Ahsahta Press, 2017.

G'Sell, Eileen. *Life After Rugby*. Gold Wake Press Collective, 2017.

Hall, Donald. *Goatfoot Milktongue Twinbird: Interviews, Essays, and Notes on Poetry, 1970–76*. University of Michigan Press, 1978.

Halliday, Mark. "Apoca-Zowie: On Traci Brimhall's Our Lady of the Ruins (Norton, 2012)." *Pleiades*, vol. 35, no. 1, winter 2015, pp. 209–210.

Harryman, Carla. *Sue in Berlin*. Mont-Saint-Aignan Cedex, Presses Universitaires de Rouen, 2018.

Helle, Anita. Review of *The Structure of Obscurity: Gertrude Stein, Language, and Cubism. MFS Modern Fiction Studies*, vol. 33 no. 4, 1987, p. 672–673. *Project MUSE*, doi:10.1353/mfs.0.1340.

Heynen, Robert, and Emily Van der Meulen. *Expanding the Gaze*. University of Toronto Press, 2016.

Hoke, Henry. *Genevieves*. Subito Press. May 1, 2017.

James, John. "Microreview: Danniel Schoonebeek, American Barricade." *Boston Review*, 2014. https://bostonreview.net/poetry-microreview/john-james-microreview-danniel-schoonebeek-american-barricade.

Jeffries, Lesley. *Textual Construction of the Female Body: A Critical Discourse Approach*. Palgrave Macmillan, 2014.

Johnston, Carol Ann. "Theorizing Typography: Printing, Page Design, and the Study of Free Verse." *The American Poetry Review*, vol. 39, no. 3, 2010, pp. 45–47.

Joshi, Priti and Susan Zieger. "Amodern 7: Ephemera and Ephemerality." Dec. 2017. https://amodern.net/article/amodern-7-ephemera-ephemerality/.

Kaminsky, Ilya. *Deaf Republic*. Gray Wolf Press, 2019.

Kaschock, Kirsten. *Confessional Sci-Fi: A Primer*. Subito Press, 2017.

Kelsey, Karla. *A Conjoined Book: Aftermath and Become Tree, Become Bird*. Omnidawn, 2014.

Kelsey, Karla. *Of Sphere*. Essay Press, 2017.

Kim, Myung Mi. Lecture delivered at SUNY Buffalo, Spring 2012 in the Poetics Program.

Konchan, Virginia. *The End of Spectacle*. Carnegie Mellon University Press, 2018.

Kristeva, Julie. *Revolution in Poetic Language*. Columbia University Press, 1985.

Irigaray, Luce. *This Sex Which Is Not One*. Cornell University Press, 1985.

Larkosh, Christopher. *Re-Engendering Translation: Transcultural Practice, Gender/ Sexuality and the Politics of Alterity*. Taylor & Francis, 2014.

Leavitt, Gracie. *Livingry*. Nightboat Books, 2018.

Lim, Dennis. "Explaining Movies by Jumping Right Inside Them." *The New York Times*, April 15, 2007. https://www.nytimes.com/2007/04/15/movies/15lim. html.

Liu, Kenji. *Monsters I Have Been*. Alice James Books, 2019.

Lugones, María. "Playfulness, 'World'-Travelling, and Loving Perception." *Hypatia*, vol. 2, no. 2, 1987, pp. 3–19.

Lyons, Elizabeth. *The Blessing of Dark Water*. Alice James Books, 2017.

Mallarmé, Stéphane. "A Throw of the Dice." University of California Press, 1994.

Map Magazine. https://mapmagazine.co.uk/

McClure, Michael. *Meat Science Essays*. City Lights Books, 1970.

Miller, Chris P. "Silence." *The Chicago School of Media Theory*, University of Chicago, 2007. https://lucian.uchicago.edu/blogs/mediatheory/keywords/silence/.

Minniti-Shippey, Jennifer. *After the Tour*. Calypso Editions, 2018.

Mohabir, Rajiv. *The Taxidermist's Cut*. Four Way Books, 2016.

Nelson, Cary. *The Oxford Handbook of Modern and Contemporary American Poetry*. Oxford University Press, 2012, p. 590.

Nguyen, Viet Thanh. "Viet Thanh Nguyen Reveals How Writers' Workshops Can Be Hostile." *The New York Times*, April 26, 2017. https://www.nytimes. com/2017/04/26/books/review/viet-thanh-nguyen-writers-workshops.html.

Olstein, Lisa. *Late Empire*. Copper Canyon Press, 2017.

Peebles, Cate. *Thicket*. Lost Roads Publishers, 2018.

Pence, Amy. *[It] Incandescent*. Ninebark Press, 2018.

Peirce, Kathleen. *Vault: A Poem*. New Michigan Press, 2017.

Powell, Elizabeth. *Concerning the Holy Ghost's Interpretation of J. Crew Catalogues*. Leaky Boot Press, 2019.

Purpura, Lia. "An Interview with Lia Purpura." *The Pinch Journal*, Oct. 2015.

Purpura, Lia. *On Looking*. Sarabande Books, 2006.

Purpura, Lia. "Relativity." "For Marvin Bell." *The Los Angeles Review of Books*, Oct. 23, 2020. https://lareviewofbooks.org/article/for-marvin-bell/.

Pound, Ezra. "A Few Dont's By An Imagiste." *Poetry: A Magazine of Verse*, 1913.

Purcell, Laura. *The Corset*. Bloomsbury Publishing, 2019.

Rasmussen, David. *Mythic-Symbolic Language and Philosophical Anthropology: A Constructive Interpretation of the Thought of Paul Ricœur*. Springer Netherlands, 1971.

Rohrer, Matthew. *The Others*. Wave Books, 2017.

Roussow, Henk. *Xamissa*. Fordham University Press, 2018.

Seguin, Andrew. *The Room in Which I Work*. Omnidawn, 2017.

Sheck, Laurie. *A Monster's Notes*. Knopf, 2012.

Sharif, Solmaz. *Look*. Graywolf Press, 2003.

Shilling, Chris. *The Body and Social Theory*. Second ed., SAGE Publications, 2003.

Sontag, Susan. *Styles of the Radical Will*. Picador, 2002.

Stonecipher, Donna. *Transaction Histories*. University of Iowa Press, 2018.

Story, Julia. *Post Moxie*. Sarabande Books, 2010.

Talusan, Grace. *The Body Papers*. Restless Books, 2019.

Tate Museum. "Art Term: Installation Art." https://www.tate.org.uk/art-terms/i/installation-art.

Terazawa, Sophia. "ephemera: A MANIFESTO for TIP 2017." The University of Arizona Poetry Center. 19 Oct 2017. https://poetry.arizona.edu/blog/ephemera-manifesto-tip-2017.

Tomash, Barbara. *Pre-*. Black Radish Books, 2018.

Wade, Julie Marie. *When I was Straight*. A Midsummer Night's Press, 2014.

Wadud, Asiya. *Crosslight for Youngbird*. Nightboat Books, 2018.

Welhouse, Abigail. "The Rumpus Interview with Victoria Chang." *The Rumpus*, Sept. 23, 2013. https://therumpus.net/2013/09/the-rumpus-interview-with-victoria-chang/.

Williams, William Carlos. *Spring and All*. Contact Publishing Co., 1923.

Winn, Sarah Ann. *Alma Almanac*. Barrow Street Press, 2017.

Wittgenstein, Ludwig. *Tractatus Logico-Philosophicus*. New York, Harcourt, Brace, & Company, 1922.

Womer, Brenna. *Atypical Cells of Undetermined Significance: Essays and Poems*. C&R Press, 2018.

Vap, Sarah. *End of the Sentimental Journey*. Noemi Press, 2013.

Veglahn, Sara. *The Ladies: A Novel*. Noemi Press, 2017.

VIDA Count. https://www.vidaweb.org/the-count/.

INDEX

Kristina Marie Darling is the author of thirty-six books, which include *Stylistic Innovation, Conscious Experience, and the Self in Modernist Women's Poetry,* forthcoming from Rowman & Littlefield Publishing Group; *Daylight Has Already Come: Selected Poems 2014–2020,* which will be published by Black Lawrence Press; *Silence in Contemporary Poetry,* which will be published in hardcover by Clemson University Press in the United States and Liverpool University Press in the United Kingdom; *Silent Refusal: Essays on Contemporary Feminist Writing,* newly available from Black Ocean; *Angel of the North,* which is forthcoming from Salmon Poetry; and *X Marks the Dress: A Registry* (co-written with Carol Guess), which was just launched by Persea Books in the United States. Penguin Random House Canada has also published a Canadian edition.

An expert consultant with the U.S. Fulbright Commission, Dr. Darling's work has also been recognized with three residencies at Yaddo, where she has held the Martha Walsh Pulver Residency for a Poet and the Howard Moss Residency in Poetry; seven residencies at the American Academy in Rome, where she has also served as an ambassador for recruitment; grants from the Elizabeth George Foundation and Harvard University's Kittredge Fund; a Fundación Valparaíso fellowship to live and work in Spain; a Hawthornden Castle Fellowship, funded by the Heinz Foundation; an artist-in-residence position at Cité Internationale des Arts in Paris; two grants from the Whiting Foundation; a Faber Residency in the Arts, Sciences, and Humanities, which she received on two separate occasions; an artist-in-residence position with the Andorran Ministry of Culture; an artist-in-residence position at the Florence School of Fine Arts; an appointment at Scuola Internazionale de Grafica in Venice; and the Dan Liberthson Prize from the Academy of American Poets, which she received on three separate occasions; among many other awards and honors. Dr. Darling serves as Editor-in-Chief of Tupelo Press & *Tupelo Quarterly.* Born and raised in the American Midwest, she currently divides her time between the United States and Europe.